The white prisoner

Galabin Boevski's secret story

Ognian Georgiev

ISBN:1500702072
ISBN-13:9781500702076

CONTENTS

CHAPTER I

Based on a true story

The pen revolved between the fingers of his right hand. There were only two sentences on the page. Galabin lifted his eyes towards the lamp above him. It wasn't bright enough, but at least it worked. There was no window in the library to give natural light. The walls were covered with shelves, full of books in Portuguese. Here and there you could find a book in English.

Galabin was in no hurry. There was one, maybe two hours until the end of the free time period. There were two other prisoners in the library. A mulatto with glasses, probably a Peruvian or Bolivian, was reading a book with a dark cover. The other one, white like him was focusing on a newspaper. He had a scar on his left cheek, left by something other than a razor.

For the umpteenth time in his life, Boevski felt oppressed. The thoughts in his head kept coming. Again

1

and again he went over the events. It has been a week since the arrest. First, he spent a night in the jail of Sao Paulo's airport, then transferred to another Brazilian prison for temporary detention. Now he was in Itai, a prison for foreigners, filled with people from all over the world. 1500 prisoners were serving their sentences here. Most of them were people like him – accused of drug trafficking. There were others – murderers, rapists, fraudsters and thieves.

"I have to do it," he thought, "I am Galabin Boevski. Olympic champion, not a mule!"

The hand that used to lift a weight of almost 200 kilograms squeezed the pen. His eyes looked at the top of the page. There, in his messy childish handwriting were two sentences. He had put everything into them:

"Mother, father, do not be ashamed of me, I have done nothing. You know me best of all!"

He felt his heart shrink. He knew the date – the 30th of October. Stella, his mother, who had raised him and supported him without question, had a birthday. His hand moved on the paper, and the thumping in his heart became stronger.

"Happy birthday, mother. This is not the best gift you have received."

***

"Boy, you have qualities, but you are short and feeble. They will push and hurt you. We are looking for bigger, stronger football players," one of the two teachers, conducting the exams for the sports school in the city of Pleven, Bulgaria was speaking in a drawl. His name was Velichko Dihonov and he had to screen about a hundred youngsters for ten vacancies.

"But comrade, look at Maradona's height, and look what he can do! I will be the second Maradona." The dark haired child replied confidently.

He was about 25 kilos, and came up to the lower part of Dihonov's back. There was no hesitation in the words he spoke. Several weeks earlier, the boy was sitting in the best seat of the house in front of the TV, watching the FIFA World Cup in Mexico '86. Maradona was at his best. The Argentinians had won the cup, and the legendary football player had scored three goals and made five assists.

"He will not get into the first grade." Dihonov told the boy's mother. "He should try for the second or third."

The thirty year old woman, dressed smartly, pursed her lips. She was short, tidy, with a kind expression on her face, but at this very moment, her stare could pierce a hole in the coach's head.

Stella and Galabin had arrived the same morning from the small town of Knezha in excellent spirits. The day was rainy, but she was sure her son would be accepted into the school. She had assurances from the football world. She was one of them. She had been the secretary of the town's football club for many years. Galabin, who had finished the fifth grade in the spring, played in the youth team. Stella knew there was no way for him to develop in Knezha. He was good, at least in his mother's eyes. There he would play only in the lower tiers – in the local championships, where legs were broken every other game.

Another man was following the tests closely. Satisfaction spread over his face, as he observed Galabin covering all the regulations. He smiled, after Velichko Dihonov turned down the boy. He had an arrangement with the football coach. Stefcho Malkodanski knew the ten positions were already filled by kids with good contacts. Even the best of the talented boys were exceeded by their parent's ambitions. Stefcho knew Stella from Knezha. He had not spoken to her, because he knew the mother's ambitions. He waited for a good time to put his offer in a kindly way.

"Hey boy, why don't you come along to the

weightlifting gym for a trial? If you pass, you can spend one year under my tutoring in weightlifting. If some position comes up in the football class, you can transfer in the second year. What about it?" Malkodanski dangled the bait.

Stella was not happy, but she saw the smile shining on her son's face again. She nodded her head and walked after Malkodanski and Galabin while she put away her umbrella.

***

About 500-600 children entered the Pleven's sport school's entrance exams every year. The open places were about 120. Exams in football and track and field were conducted first, because most of the kids applied for them. The exams for wrestling and weightlifting were last.

The boys were being tested one after another on the bars in the gym. Galabin was among them. Stefcho Malkodanski was already certain he had the boy he was interested in. He didn't let the mother out of his sight.

The air in the gym stank of sweat, and Stella's head was filled with various thoughts. She watched Galabin as he stood gazing at the round weights. Bad feelings came into her mind. Stella and Peppy, his father, were worried Galabin was too short for his age. They wondered, even though there were no tall people in their families. Galabin's sister – Tanya was also short. Her boy was too small and fragile to be a weightlifter, just like her husband's favourite pigeons, the boy was named after[1].

"Stefcho, what if my son never gets any taller? I have never seen a tall weightlifter," Stella asked.

"Don't worry," Malkodanski said in his magical voice, "there are heavy categories, where the weightlifters are

---

[1] The name Galabin comes from Galab, which is the Bulgarian word for Pigeon.

quite tall."

While they talked, Galabin decided to try the weights. The bar had 20 kilograms on it. Malkodanski was busy calming Stella, and too late saw what the mischievous boy was doing. The kid lifted the bar, turned it, but the weight pushed him down and he fell on his back. The barbell trapped him. The boy screamed with all his might. Everyone in the gym gathered around. Stefcho and Stella set Galabin free. The boy was fine.

"Come on, let's leave," Stella gave instructions as she seized her umbrella that had been thrown down moments earlier. "Did you see what happened? Take your things we are going to get the bus."

The tears were still wet on Galabin's face. The boy stood up, but moved no further. He was looking at the barbell. He took two steps and set it straight, in the position he tried to lift it from.

"No, I will be an athlete. I am staying here. You leave. I am not going anywhere," the child replied bravely.

"It's good your father is not here! Then we would see if you would have stayed!" Stella raised her voice, gently reminding him of his father's heavy hand.

Peppy was a legend in the district's builder brigades. One of the best steelworkers in the area. The calluses on his hands were more than the number of rakias[2] the biggest drunk in Knezha could drink.

"If I can't attend the sports school, I won't go to school at all. I have told everyone in Knezha I am going to Pleven," Galabin bristled.

He was certain he would get what he wanted. He would not move an inch back from his mother's threats. He knew it would be more difficult at home, so he had to win her over to his side.

---

[2] Rakia is Bulgaria's brandy, national and high – alcohol drink. Rakias means as well glasses full with Rakia.

Stefcho Malkodanski understood the delicate situation. It was all or nothing. Right here, in the weightlifting gym was going to be decided the fate of the little boy. The teacher understood two things. The boy had character. It was quite rare, during those years for a kid to oppose his mother in front of other people. A slap or beating with a stick often followed. After that there was the father's heavy hand, which sometimes held a belt. Similar punishments acted as discipline for the younger generation to respect their elders.

Malkodanski was thinking of something else too. Even if he took the child, it would be bound to cause trouble in the future. He was too wild, self-confident and primitive. He would not let anybody give him orders.

"Let's not argue here," the mother's tone softened. "We will go home and think about it. If you want to be an athlete so much – be one. But your father has to approve it."

Galabin smiled and looked at the barbell again. He had already encountered one in Knezha, a while back. One day he passed through the gym by accident, with a couple of friends. Inside he was noticed by the world champion Pavlin Kakrinski who by chance, was an acquaintance of Malkodanski.

"Stefcho, there is a boy in Knezha, with great proportions for a weightlifter," Kakrinski had remarked a couple of months ago. "I wanted him to try the weights, but he refused – he was going to apply for football at your school."

The wily teacher had played his hand well. He knew the battle was won. While he was walking with Stella and Galabin he decided to play his last card.

"Galabin, do you want to come to the school's summer camp? You will meet the other kids. It is ten days of games and workouts. You will love it."

"Stefcho, do not rush into this," his mother interfered. "Let's see what Peppy has to say. He may not agree that our son should spend his energy on the weights."

"Yes, of course," Maklodanski backed off. "It is not certain I will be able to take him to the camp, because he is not our student yet."

"I am going!" Galabin said without even looking at his mother.

"I will ask permission from the school principal – Nikolay Sabev," Maklodanski said seriously, and at the same time, he wanted to hug himself on the successful completion of the mission. "I don't think there will be a problem."

***

Weightlifting is a strange and difficult sport. The weightlifters work for one or two important competitions during the year. Everyone's eyes are set on the European or World Championships. The Olympics are once every four years. Failure is very painful, because the weightlifters don't have a chance for a repeat and have to wait months for the next battle on the stage.

Years ago, there were three events in weightlifting, but now there are only two. The first one is called "the snatch", and the second "the clean and jerk". The competitors have three attempts. They choose the weights themselves. If the weightlifter fails in either of the two events he receives a "zero" and is disqualified for the total competition.

The champion is determined by the total of weights lifted in the snatch and the clean and jerk. If there is a tie in scores, the winner is the physically lighter competitor.

***

"No way!" Peppy Boevski grunted, while breaking a large piece of bread. "I will not support that. What weightlifter could he be? Look how skinny he is. His arms are like sticks. He is less than 25 kilos. Couldn't you have picked a different sport? Do you see me doing fine needlework, for example, with these rough hands?"

Stella stood silent for a moment. She knew it was the best tactic. If she said anything, there would be fierce retaliation. Galabin was outside. He was playing in the yard, already certain he would start school in Pleven, that September.

"I don't want him to be a weightlifter too, but how can he qualify in football, when all leaders of the Communist

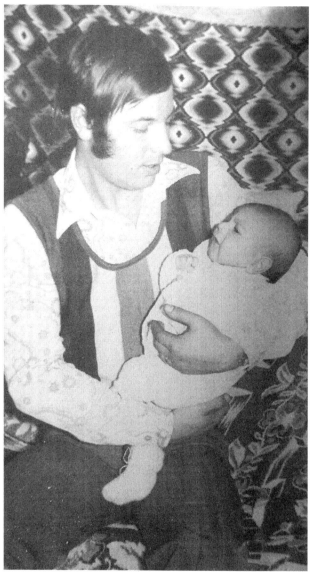

Father Pepi and baby Galabin

Party want their sons to be like Goondy and Iakimov[3]," Stella replied, while cleaning a plate, that was filled with bean soup minutes earlier. She put a new one with hot stuffed peppers in front of him.

"You don't know how things are. They promised he would be accepted in football, but he turned out to be too short and skinny. What a load of rubbish! He passed the tests without any trouble. I have an agreement with Malkodanski – Galabin will be a weightlifter in the first year. He will gain some strength. In the second year, when the sons of the party leaders drop out, he will step in, and continue in football."

Stella was sitting at the table, watching her husband devour his supper. He wanted the best for his kid, and he would not make him a steelworker or a farmer, like most of the people in Knezha.

"Athlete... athlete...," Peppy continued. "How did he came up with that? He could go to a technical school, he could have a profession. But let him do it! Let him bang his head against the wall. I don't see him getting very far with it. When he grows strong, the best he could become is a labourer.

Stella knew she had won. Or lost. She remembered the 20 kilogram barbell. What if it has fallen on his head? She would not dwell on it. She would suffer in silence and pray Galabin stayed safe and sound. Let him get through the first year, the second will be different in the football class.

***

Malkodanski was overseeing another workout in the gym. Young Galabin was forging ahead of the rest of the

---

[3] Andrey Asparuhov – Goondy and Dimitar Yakimov are legendary Bulgarian football players from the sixties and seventies of the twentieth century.

The kid was too small and fragile to be a weightlifter in his first years

boys. It was as though he was setting goals for himself in everything he did. He followed most of the coach's instructions. He knew he had to eat well to gain weight. The lightest category was up to 44 kilos, and in one year he gained up to 32-33 kilograms. He also grew ten centimeters taller. His hands still looked skinny, but he gained a lot of muscles in his legs. This was the most important thing for a weightlifter. Nothing could be achieved in this sport, without a strong base.

"He is very persistent and hardworking this one," Stefcho addressed his colleague from the football class Velichko Dohonov. "You should know I made a promise to him and his mother. I don't want to lie to them. That's why I'm talking to you. The boy has a good future as a weightlifter."

"You know how it is in our department. There is always some big shot who pushes us to take his son," Dihonov replied. Several years later he would become the executive director of football club Litex and lead them to win the Bulgarian championship. "Even if I wanted to, I would not be able to take him in."

Malkodanski was pleased by the way things had worked out. He knew the boy's attitude towards the barbell has changed. He would always set goals for himself, higher than the ones his coach has set. He could concentrate and control himself in the gym. Most of his peers were entering puberty and their minds were occupied with different things. The teacher was aware of everything. He knew nobody succeeds in the weightlifting world without total concentration. This was the reason Galabin's scores were so good. Malkodanski couldn't wait to let him compete. But the rules were clear and the boy wasn't old enough.

When he started at the sports school Galabin was living with his grandparents in Pleven. Stella's parents had an apartment on the other side of the town. The boy had to walk a long way every day.

Unlike his classmates he didn't have a place to rest between school and workouts. There was no point in trying to go back to the apartment, it was too far away, and time was short.

"Mum, I want you to move me to the school dormitory," Galabin said to Stella. "I have no time to prepare for classes."

The woman finally understood her son had chosen his career on the first of May. For the holiday, after the mandatory Communist parade, their family's friends gathered in Knezha to have a party, and let the kids play. The merrymaking in the house was not to Galabin's taste. He had just come home from Pleven. Galabin asked his mother to drive him to the gym. There was no one there. Just him, the barbell and the weights.

***

"Come immediately," Stella read the telegram. She showed it to Peppy, and worrying thoughts rushed through her head. The decision was taken in seconds. Galabin's parents left for the resort village of Michurin. They left their daughter Tanya with friends.

Galabin and his sister Tanya are riding a bear

"Everything happens at these sea camps," thought Stella, who now had high blood pressure, and felt like everything was falling apart. "I hope it's not bad news. I knew we shouldn't have left him alone. He is too young."

Several hours later the parents arrived at the children's camp. Kids were playing everywhere, and nothing in the happy noise indicated, that something had happened to Galabin.

"Have you seen him?" Stella's question was directed at her son's classmate Ivan Ivanov from Dolni Dabnik. The boy was one of Galabin's best friends.

"He was around, there is comrade Malkodanski, he will explain," Ivan pointed.

Malkodanski approached in his shorts, his belly protruding from his t-shirt. By his smile Stella understood nothing had happened to her boy.

"Stefcho what is all this in the telegram? You scared the wits out of us!" The mother asked abruptly.

"I am very sorry, Stella, I didn't mean to frighten you," the teacher excused himself in a pleasant manner. "You have to sign a declaration, that you will let him participate in a competition in the Soviet Union. He is still a minor, and the rules require it."

At this moment Galabin showed up, breathless from the games. Stella took a good look at him, just to put an end to her worries. The boy had darkened and grown in his two years at the school. He was no longer her little boy, who once could have been blown away by the Danube valley's strong winds.

"Galabin, go and play a bit more, your parents and I need a word," Malkodanski's voice interrupted Stella's thoughts. "Look, I will admit I want him to compete in the next national championship."

Stella wasn't very up to date with the championships, but she knew her child was too young.

"He isn't fourteen yet, this is why I am going to fake his identity card. It's a harmless fraud, and the child is ready to win," Malkodansky added. "He wants to implement the things he is achieving in his workouts. I can't stop him."

Peppy, the father, looked at Stella. He shook his head and refused to think of the stupid competitions. He still couldn't believe that any good would come of the hundreds of hours spent in the gym.

"Alright, we will let him go," Stella said quietly, looking at Galabin's back, which was receding further and further away from her.

CHAPTER II

„Acordais, acordais"[4] the guard was shouting while banging on the bars. Galabin had been awake for a while now. He didn't need extra help with it. He acquired that habit from his time at the prestigious sport school "Olympic Hopes", and after that at the national team's camps. He would never forget the punctuality of the legendary weightlifting coach Ivan Abadzhiev. Everybody called the coach Senior Trainer or Abadzhiata. The specialist not only woke up his athletes, but also turned off the lights in the evening. Sometimes after three heavy workouts per day, Galabin got back to his room fifteen minutes before midnight, dead beat and still sweaty. He and his teammate Georgi Gardev, didn't have enough strength left to go to the bathroom and take a shower. Time passed, and the two of them were still lying down with their strength drained. Exactly at midnight Abadzhiata used to enter the room and turn off the lights. Without saying a word. Senior Trainer was always punctual and used to punish everyone who was late. He didn't care

---

[4] Get up, get up (Portugal).

16

that by the time Galabin and his teammates recovered after his killer workouts, it would be two in the morning.

The noise from the running shower and water in the tank pouring down the toilet brought him back to reality. The fast speech in African dialects and Spanish phrases were a morning tradition in the miserable cell. It should have been for six prisoners, but there were twelve instead. Galabin was one of them. He had no luck and ended up in a cell where all beds were taken. His spot was on the ground. The cold from the floor passed through the mat every night.

He couldn't sleep well for the first week. He woke up at the slightest noise and had trouble falling back to sleep. The food in the prison was not the best. The prisoners with weak guts and junkies, most of all, passed wind. The smell didn't pose a big problem. It was one of the first things they got used to. The cold also. The worst thing was waiting for the bathroom and toilet. Quarrels often broke out over who was the first to go in. His cellmates were divided into groups of two or three men. He was alone, like a wolf. As always. The others respected him. They found out quickly that he was an Olympic champion. They sensed something tough in him. And this was not Galabin's first time in a jungle like this one, where you can survive only by protecting your rights at all times.

***

Galabin was hanging from the ninth floor's balcony upside down. Two strong wrestler's hands were holding his legs, and were the only reason that he did not fall down. The boy from Knezha felt the fear of death for the first time in his life. Not being very good at physics, he calculated the ground could be very far and very close at the same time.

A wrestler from a higher grade has crept up on him in the corridors of the "Olympic hopes" boarding school.

Galabin didn't know how to react and was thrown over the railing in seconds. He made a noise, which wasn't a cry for help. He decided to be silent, no matter what. He quickly understood, that the only man who could help him was the one holding his legs. There was only one thing he could do – to ask himself how he ended up there.

***

He had just got into the prestigious sports school "Olympic Hopes" in Sofia. The coaches in the school were gathering the most talented young Bulgarians from the whole country. They watched them at competitions. They estimated their potential and tried to persuade the parents and the teachers in their current schools.

Emilyan Yankov was one of the people doing the selection. This was his last time, because he, like a lot of other Bulgarian coaches was looking for a career abroad, after the fall of communism in 1989. He had noticed young Boevski's achievements one year before heading to the USA.

"He will remain your athlete, but he will have a lot better chance to grow there with the best of Bulgaria's talent," Emilyan Yankov turned to the sceptical Stefcho Malkodanski. "You have to understand it would be very beneficial to him. The national team trains alongside us. He will become even more inspired, by watching big names, like Nikolay Peshalov, Alexander Varbanov, Stefan Botev…

Malkodanski wasn't sure. He knew how they stole athletes from the clubs in the country and then no one remembered their first trainers. Galabin had already started to display his potential. He was doing well.

"I don't know, You shall have to speak to his parents," the wily coach replied, remembering how hard it was to persuade Stella a few years back. "If it was up to me he would go. I can keep an eye on him from here and always be there to guide him."

***

The hot coffee was steaming, but its aroma could not distract Emilyan Yankov. He knew every word counted.

"Our goal is to prepare these kids for the national team. They have to represent the country," the coach from "Olympic Hopes" still used this love for the country, which used to be emphasized daily by the Communists.

Stella had received the stranger from Sofia in the family house. She already knew Galabin's opinion. She could sense, from her son's words, that Pleven was already too small for him. The 15-year-old student had grown up. There were several gold medals in his room already.

"His father and I are against it," the mother answered in her typical, straightforward way. "Sofia is a big city. Life is different there. We won't be able to see him, because it's too far. And we don't have any relatives who could help him, if something happens."

Yankov understood it was time to change tactics. He looked at Galabin and decided to concentrate his efforts on the boy. It was a still fragile kid who was sitting in front of him. There were no muscles on his arms, usual for weightlifters, but the coach from Sofia knew they were as tough as boat ropes. His legs looked sturdy. With his sharp awareness he guessed the dark haired boy was very emotional.

"Galabin, for many kids from all over Bulgaria it is an honour to attend our school," Yankov started to implement his strategy developed for attracting talent. "From your teacher Stefcho Malkodanski I found out there was no room for you in the sports school at first. But you have proven yourself, and you no longer have to beg. Quite the opposite – we are inviting you."

"Yes, I will go," the boy said firmly without taking his eyes off the coach. "Mum, don't worry. I have been living in a school dormitory for three years now. I doubt if Sofia would be very different. Since I will know nobody I will be less distracted and put more time and effort into my training."

Stella shook her head. She knew there was no way to stop her son.

"Have it your way," she stopped and wondered if the family suitcase that, they used for vacations, would be big enough for the boy's clothes.

***

"It was all a joke, new boy. You didn't think I was going to let you go, did you?" The wrestler was laughing at Galabin, who was leaning over the railing.

Little Boevski was clenching his teeth. He could not feel his legs, and was afraid to get up, because he might collapse on the floor again. They had pulled him back up a minute ago. He didn't remember how much time he had been hanging upside down. But he knew who did it, and he would never forget him.

The counsellors and coaches never found out about the incident. Things like that happened every day. It was rare for someone to complain even for those who got hurt. Those who did wouldn't finish the three years in the jungle called "Olympic Hopes".

***

The regime in "Olympic Hopes" was Spartan. And so were the living conditions. At the end of 1989 and the beginning of 1990 you could sense the coming collapse. Coaches and counsellors were saying in the evenings, over a glass of rakia and Shopska salad[5], that the days of the

---

[5] Traditional Bulgarian salad with tomatoes, cucumbers, peppers and white cheese.

Boevski started to win medals from a young age

unique intern school were numbered. Despite the hunger, the power and water cuts, the inflation and the reduced interest of the young generation in sports, the school lasted until the middle of the 90's.

The talented boy from Knezha was living with the other weightlifters and the cyclists on the 13th floor. Two storeys up were the wrestlers. Several years earlier the future bosses of Bulgaria's underworld shared rooms there – the brothers Vasil and Georgi Ilievi, Mladen Mihalev – Madzho, Ilia Pavlov. The 16th floor was occupied by the boxers.

Nine students were living in each apartment. There were three rooms. There were beds, bedside tables and a wardrobe. Nobody complained. On the contrary, manhood was being forged in conditions like these. The food was good, the teachers – excellent specialists, and the training was extremely hard but beneficial.

Each morning the future national athletes were woken up at 6:30. Classes started after breakfast at 7:15. The first weightlifting training in the gym began at 10:00 and lasted until 12:30. Then they had lunch, and went back to school. The last part of the day was toughest - the afternoon training, which lasted from 16:30 until 19:00. The only free time they had was in the evening. The doors were locked dead on 21:00.

"What happens if we don't get back in time?" asked one of Galabin's closest friends and future World and European champion Stefan "The Lizard" Georgiev in his first week in "Olympic Hopes". He got his nickname from his early years in the "Locomotive" (Sofia) sports school.

"First – you will sleep outside. Second – you pack your bags and go back to where you came from," was the answer of the other weightlifting coach and ex competitor Tzviatko Petkov

There were no classes during the weekend. But the future national athletes were having a training session in the weightlifting gym. There were about 35 weightlifters from all classes. In Emilyan Yankov's group were The Lizard, Yoto Yotov and Plamen Zhelyazkov – all future heroes on world and European stages. Under Tzviatko Petkov was being trained Yany Marchkov "Marchocka", who became one of Galabin's best friends.

The boys' self-esteem was growing daily. They admired the lifters at the gym next door, where the national athletes were training under the supervision of Norair Nurikyan.

"You boys have the chance to stand 40-50 meters away from the champions that bring glory to Bulgaria," Emilyan Yankov was hyping up his students after training. "To be able to walk the path between the two gyms you have to lift about 40-50 more kilos than you do at present."

***

The phone rang for a long time. Galabin had promised to speak to his mother once a week. He picked up the phone and heard Stella's familiar, worried voice.

"How are you my boy, do they feed you ok?" Stella asked 170 kilometers away in the northeast of the country. She had already been in Sofia to inspect the intern school. She wasn't very impressed.

"It's nice mum, don't you and dad worry. It's not a lot different than Pleven," Galabin answered routinely. He had no intention in sharing the bad things. He knew it would worry his already troubled mother more.

"You are coming home for the spring break, right? Tanya has grown so much, you won't recognize her," Stella changed the subject, while imagining herself covering the table with Galabin's favourite dishes, without realizing that he had to keep to the weight for his category.

"I can't wait. I get tired of the steel bars too, you know," young Boevski replied, to calm his ever-watchful parent.

***

In Bulgaria only five or six weightlifters had become masters of the sport before turning sixteen. The honourable title was awarded for a good result. It was adopted from the Soviet Union and craved by every athlete. It was Galabin's first goal after he started at "Olympic Hopes".

"Are you sure you want this? Why don't you hold off for a while?" Tzviatko Petkov asked rhetorically. He had taken over the group from Emilian Yankov, who left for the USA.

"I can't participate in the men's competitions anyway, but at least let me do this," Galabin replied, eager to prove himself on the stage after many years of heavy training.

In the national championship the talented boy received permission to try for the rank Master of sport. Galabin participated individually out of competition. He did it without any trouble and gained the respect of his classmates. No one was messing with him anymore.

***

The disco in Knezha was full of teenagers. The fashion for long hair and short skirts had not passed this part of Bulgaria by. With the dawn of democracy western music hits finally replaced Bulgarian artists. The stars CC Catch, Sandra and Madonna were competing against the Serbian kings and queens of pop-folk Lepa Brena, Vesna Zmijanach and Miroslav Ilich in the DJ's playlists.

Galabin knew that the only time he could party was during the break. At other times he preferred to rest after the heavy training.

The sixteen-year-old weightlifter was not one of the tallest boys, but he was brawny. He glanced at the dancing girls while pulling confidently on his cigarette. He learned to smoke in the sports school

His eyes fell on a slim girl with a ponytail. Galabin fell in love within seconds. He didn't go up to her straightaway. He got his cousin, who was also the pretty girl's classmate to help him. The beauty's name was Krasimira.

When Galabin returned to "Olympic Hopes" the only thing to keep him warm were Krasi's letters.

***

Everybody in the cafeteria was looking in one direction. Galabin is hitting and kicking a classmate in the head. The boy is older than him, but he pays for his sins nonetheless. He was the one who hanged the weightlifter from the ninth floor a year earlier. He had decided to continue the bullying, but this time he met opposition.

Galabin holds his own. The wrestler pays the higher price. He gets a thick ear. The score is settled. What goes around comes around is a law in "Olympic Hopes".

***

"This is unacceptable, you are not living in a jungle!" The principal Dzherikarov shouts in a strict voice. He is a sports person. He knows what it is to live in an environment like that. "Do you have something to say for yourself about the fight?"

"I don't, comrade," Galabin replies clearly.

"You are lucky we are not under Communist rule anymore. Then I would not have been able to save you even if you were Naim Suleymanoglu," the principal shakes his head. He knew this was the worst punishment he could enforce for a first offence – scolding. Expulsion from "Olympic Hopes" was very rare, regardless of the student's poor grades outside the gyms. "This is your last chance!"

***

A tense silence hangs in the air in the principal's office. There are two other people in there, besides Galabin and comrade Dzherikarov.

"It was them, comrade, I saw them," one of the teachers in the school points his finger at Boevski and Marchocka. "These rascals slashed my car's tyres."

"Is that true?" the principal asks the future national athletes.

Marchoka and Galabin remained silent. They don't even look at each other. They haven't conspired. They trust each other, as they trust all of their classmates in "Olympic Hopes". They took revenge on the teacher for telling on them, when he saw them smoking.

"I am so disappointed in you, Galabin. Both you and Yany know smoking is forbidden. And damaging private property is just unacceptable. I warned you. I don't have any other choice, but to expel you," Dzherikarov said firmly.

***

The teacher's council was convened to decide the fate of Boevski and Marchocka. The one who slashed the tyres had conspired with his colleagues. The teachers were determined to teach the vandals discipline once and for all. The two weightlifters had the silent support of their coaches, who had been down the same path. The votes were unbalanced, because there were more teachers and staff than coaches. Galabin and Marchocka were expelled.

***

"Stella, come to Pleven. Don't worry, but it is important," Malkodanski's voice sounded mysterious.

"Is there trouble at school? Are we being expelled from Pleven too?" Galabin's mother did not avoid the question.

"No, nothing like that. Everything is fine at school. You go to my place, we will come along after training," Malkodanski finished.

Galabin was back from Sofia attending the eleventh grade in the good old sports school in Pleven. He used to spend a lot of time in Knezha, where he started training with his uncle Hristo Boev. The two of them quickly found a common language. They were good together in training. Officially, the coach was still Stefcho Malkodanski, who also kept close contact with him.

Stella was keeping her son on a short leash, ever since he returned from Sofia. Her mother's instinct indicated something had happened, but could not guess what by Stefcho and Galabin's looks.

"Well, what can I say, you are going to be a grandmother," the coach said bluntly.

"A grandmother?"

"Galabin is going to marry."

"What do you mean he is going to marry?"

"Well, Krasi is pregnant."

Stella was sitting down, but she held onto the sofa with her hands nonetheless. Galabin was seventeen years old, and the girl was sixteen. She, herself, was thirty-six.

"Women my age have babies, and I am going to be a grandmother," The mother thought, not being happy at all. There wasn't a lot of time to hesitate, let alone choose. They weren't going to leave the girl on her own. After all, the reason was inside her, it wasn't her fault.

"What if something like this happens to my daughter, and no one wants her?" She asked herself and the decision was made.

A couple of days later Galabin went to the pregnant Krasimira's house. He knocked on the door and asked for her hand, traditionally, from her parents. In August 1992 Galabin's first child was born – Paul. He had the first letter from his grandfather's name – Peppy. A month after the happy day, the weightlifter was called up.

***

The red Zhiguli[6] was traveling at 145km/h. Approaching the city of Sandanski the driver Stefcho Malkodanski saw the traffic policeman with his stop sign raised.

"What a blow!" the coach grunted.

On the back seat were Galabin and two more weightlifters from the sport school – Biser Uzunov and Simeon Slavov. On the front seat, snoring lightly was Gen. Bozhil Bozhilov.

"How can you drive at this speed?! Where are you going with these kids?" The officer asked.

"Officer," Malkodanski starts speaking in an elegant manner as he sees a traffic offence coming his way. "We are going to a competition in the city of Solun. The Greek embassy was a little late with our visas. We received them at noon, and we have to be there by eight for the technical conference, or we won't be allowed to participate."

"Athletes or no athletes you will get a ticket," the officer says firmly, not long ago everybody would have called him "comrade policeman".

"What seems to be the problem?" The off-duty general awakens. He is commander of the Construction Corps for northern Bulgaria and shows his military I.D.

"Oh, general, sir, I am sorry," the traffic cop straightens up. "Just for you to know, generals have road accidents too."

"Off you go, we are late for the competition," General Bozhilov ends the conversation.

In Greece the happy band gets lost. Malkodansky looks

---

[6] Automobile manufactured in the Soviet Union.

at a sign saying "Thessaloniki" and does not understand. He asks a local policeman where Solun[7] is.

"Don't say the word "Solun" here. Thessaloniki is Solun," he explains.

Galabin and the other two boys win gold medals. The general weeps like a child. The Zhiguli heads back home and arrives in Pleven thirty minutes before midnight. The tired boys step out of the car and are arrested by military police on the spot. Bozhilov smiles and tells his subordinates to take it easy.

"It is all right, just take them back to the barracks[8], because they have their oath of allegiance tomorrow. I don't want them escaping to a party somewhere."

***

The next day Galabin has his picture taken for his military I.D., gives the oath at eight in the morning and waits for Malkodanski to get him out of the barracks. Next to him is Svetlio Barkanichkov, who will years later become famous as the athlete who slept with five hundred women.

"When will they take us out?" Galabin turns to the smiling Barkanichkov.

"I don't know about you, but they promised I will be out before noon."

Exactly at ten o'clock Barkanichkov, the smart fellow, leaves the Construction Corps' barracks. Galabin sees Malkodanski, who comes to free him at five in the

---

[7] Ages ago the city of Thessaloniki was Bulgarian and had the name of Solun.

[8] Until 2007 military service was mandatory for every Bulgarian boy who graduated from grade school. The length of service varied from six months to two years.

afternoon.

"Come on, coach, Svetlio was let out in the morning. Why are you keeping me here?" Galabin asks with his fists clenched.

"Do not worry, this is your last time. You won't be coming back here. I have arranged for you a monthly military salary of twenty two levs[9]."

***

The sound of falling weights echoes through Knezha's gym. The sweaty longhaired youngster is happy with the training as is his uncle, called by the young weightlifter Big Brother. It's not been long since the two of them began to work together, but the results are amazing.

"Big Brother, I see no point in going to Pleven to train," Galabin says in a calm voice, even though the thought had been in his head for a while. "I feel better here. It's calmer for me, and Krasi and Paul are close."

"Galabin, you are Pleven's competitor," Hristo Boev replies. "You are serving there, they may cause trouble for you. Now you are about to get in the national youth team. You have a European championship at the end of the year. Things can go wrong."

"Do you want to train me? Look how much better I'm lifting lately," The boy points out his progress.

In the first months of 1993, Boevski improved considerably on his best results. He was ready for the 64 kilograms category, where the legendary champion Naim Suleymanoglu was competing. He was still far off the Turk, but he was hitting 125 kg in the snatch and 150 kg in the clean and jerk.

"Alright, I will see what I can do, but I want you to be very strict and do exactly what I say," said Hristo Boev in

[9] Bulgarian currency. At that time two levs was worth one dollar.

his slow and heavy voice, while Galabin was preparing for his next attempt.

*****

"You can have him, but you have to pay a transfer fee!" Redfaced Stefcho Malkodanski exploded. "We have invested so much money in his development – we fed and cared for him. He was sleeping in the school's dormitory. I took him to competitions.You can't just take him like that!"

"Who ever heard of a transfer in weightlifting?" Hristo Boev was shocked. "He is not Stoichkov or Penev[10]. Let's help the boy. He wants to be close to Krasi and the baby. Put yourself in his place."

"50 000 levs and not a cent less!" Stefcho Malkodanski hit the table. "I can't stop him, but we can compensate the club. With the money I will take the others to competitions.

Hristo sighed. He knew he couldn't find that much money. There was no ticket revenue in weightlifting. The government sometimes gave money to the Olympic, World, and European medalists among seniors. Galabin was only eighteen years old. He hadn't competed in any of those.

"Fine, give me a week, we will speak to each other then," Hristo Boev made up his mind.

They got the money together with the help of some businessmen from Knezha – including the brothers Marius and Spas from the Oils Factory. Galabin's uncle was wondering if he had made the best of the worst deal in his life.

---

[10] Hristo Stoichkov and Lyuboslav Penev were the best Bulgarian football players at that time.

***

The junior team's coach Ivan Lechev sees Galabin's awesome qualities and draws him in. Knezha's lion finds himself in "Dianabad" again, where he was kicked out two years earlier for slashing tyres. The childish games are only a memory, the heavy work in the gym and the year's prime goal occupy Galabin's whole attention.

In the beautiful Spanish city of Valencia in 1993, Galabin suffers the first disappointment of his career. He left very well prepared and ready to become European champion in the 64 kg category. Instead he finished sixth, achieving 127.5 kg and 150 kg in both events.

"I will keep him in a camp. He has great qualities, but he needs more competition to prepare for the big stage," said Ivan Lechev to Hristo Boev on the telephone. "Time is on his side, things will work out fine."

"I hope he is not causing you any trouble," Hristo Boev asked, because he knew all too well what happened at "Olympic Hopes."

"He is a little stubborn in the gym, but he gets through the weekly programme," Ivan Lechev explained. "I haven't seen him take alcohol, or cruise the pubs. For example I regularly have to take Sevdalin Minchev, Petar Petrov and Stefan Georgiev out of the disco club "Strong 205", owned by Tzviatko Petkov.

***

Even the healthiest man on the planet can get ill and die in Kuala Lumpur. The brutal humidity wrecked all Bulgarian weightlifters, waiting for two days in this hellhole for the plane for Jakarta, where the World Junior Championships were to be held in July, 1994. The conditions affected everybody. Stefan Georgiev lifted first in the 54 kg category. He started very well and got the silver medal. The only one ahead of him was a Chinese, who destroyed his competitors and lifted a total of 20 kg more than The Lizard.

There were great expectations in the next category – 59 kg, Sevdalin Minchev showed terrific results in training, but failed in Jakarta. He came fifth.

The national team coach was worried, and wondered what was going on. Galabin Boevski's category is coming up – 64 kg. There is one more Bulgarian in the competition – Petar "The Bone" Petrov. Everything starts perfectly. After the snatch Petar "The Bone" is first with 142.5 kg Galabin is second with 137.5 kg, but fouled at a higher weight, which he used to crush in training.

With his second lift at clean and jerk Petrov does 162.5 kg, Boevski does just as well at the first attempt.

"Galabin, do a couple more attempts on the warm up, you will get cold. Look how many people are in front of you," Ivan Lechev instructs him before the second attempt, in which Galabin will go for the title.

"There is no need. I will beat them the way I am. Look how well the clean and jerk went. I will become World Champion at my next attempt.

Galabin is confident, because he had reached up to 170 kg in training. He asks for 167.5 kg. If he clears it, he will be tied with Petar "The Bone", who has finished his attempts. Galabin has two more. If one of them is successful, he will become World Champion. The red light for an unsuccessful lift flashes. Then one more time. The competition is over. Galabin leaves the stage with his head down. He has finished fourth, and his rival for a place in the national team – Petar "The Bone" is the champion.

**

"That was it, everything is over," Galabin frets as he passes the lighter to Stefan Georgiev. "They won't include me in the national team. Damn it, what happened to me?"

"It must have been that cursed humidity," The Lizard replies, while he lights his smoke. "Don't worry yet, you have European Championships in October."

"But who would take me there?", Galabin exhales a large puff of smoke. "It's my mistake. I was confused by the good results I had while training. I should have listened to Lechev and stayed warmed up."

"Lechev is OK, you know, he is aware of how hard you prepare. He senses these things. He will take you to the European Championships."

***

The noise at "Sofia" airport was stronger than ever. The national weightlifting junior team was leaving for Rome. All the boys were exchanging last minute advice with their personal coaches and relatives. Only Galabin is sitting on his suitcase. He feels he is becoming ill. Standing over him Hristo Boev looks concerned. The autumn flu has not passed him by.

"Big Brother, look what happened because of losing weight. My immune system has collapsed."

"Lechev thinks you have to compete in the 64 kg. category. This will be your last. Then we are going for 69 kg

***

In the Eternal city the battle for the title is between Galabin and Petar "The Bone". Petrov repeats the result he did on the snatch from the World Championships in Jakarta – 142.5 kg Boevski lifts 2.5 kg less than the previous competition – 135 kg. The boy from Knezha doesn't feel well. His body's temperature is 40 degrees. He knows it will be very difficult to win the title. The good thing is there is no one else in the competition comes even close to the two Bulgarians.

The result of the clean and jerk is a tie – 162.5 kg - the first medal for Galabin from a major championship – silver. He is disappointed, because this is the second competition he has finished behind Petar "The Bone".

In two months time Galabin will turn 20 years old and will not be able to compete in the junior's anymore. He will have to lift in the men's, where the competition is twice as brutal.

CHAPTER III

This time he was alone. On the left were pages with Portuguese words. He had begun to learn the language. Knowledge was encouraged and was one more way to get out of the overcrowded cell. He also had a meeting with the attorney. It was very difficult to talk to him. He gave up trying to persuade him, that he was innocent. He decided to focus on the facts. The cursed suitcases were damaged beyond recognition after the confiscation. That was all he could understand, and these were the facts he had to use to defend himself.

He turned his head sidewards, inhaled deeply and reached for the pencil. The champion pulled out a blank page, and imagined Myra smiling. A couple of weeks ago she turned four years old. The child was probably asking where her Daddy was. The lines on the paper joined up. Dots, lines and twirls appeared on the round face. This would be the princess. Butterflies flew around her. They were easier to draw. Galabin paid attention to every detail. He knew he was no artist, but he applied himself. He wrote a few words. Myra couldn't read, but his wife Krasi and elder daughter Sarah would help.

The small, gentle girl loved to cuddle up to her father,

ever since she was a toddler. Galabin carried her around on the nights she had colic. Sometimes for an hour. Other times two. He used to feel like crying out of helplessness, because he could not stop the baby's pain. That is the worst feeling of them all. Being helpless, while the events around you make you cry.

***

Yordan Ivanov had gathered together the full squad of the senior national team. It was time for debriefing.

The competition was extremely hard. In the lightest division – 54 kg, the Olympic champion from Barcelona '92, Ivan Ivanov, and Galabin's classmate from "Olympic Hopes", Stefan "The Lizard" Georgiev, were in close competition. In the next category was Sevdalin Minchev and the three-time World champion Nikolay Peshalov, they tied the trials. Petar "The Bone" was favourite for the title in the 64 kg, after his excellent results last year. Other people in the gym were Radostin "The Penny" Dimitrov, Plamen Bratoychev, Metin Kadir and Zlatan Vanev. They were the stars in the world of weightlifting.

They all knew it would be more difficult to get in Bulgaria's team squad for the European Championships in Warsaw, than win a medal there.

Galabin was calm. He had been training constantly after the European Junior Championships in Rome last year. He spent a lot of time in the gym with his uncle Hristo Boev. His results were improving rapidly. The most important thing was, that technically the talented sportsman from Knezha was way above his peers.

***

"Big Brother, look what I have done in training. I beat Petar "The Bone" by ten kilograms, but everything is different in competition?" Galabin asked, surprisingly quickly, his trainer, one month before going to camp with the senior team.

"Man, your time will come," Boev replied slowly, as he watched Galabin put up 175 kg for the clean and jerk. Earlier he had snatched 145 kg. "Be persistent. I promise you this is not your limit. Here in Knezha you eat like an ordinary man. You don't take vitamins. We have one workout a day. The bigger weights have yet to come. You will improve your score."

Galabin remembered these words. He didn't stop repeating them during Yordan Ivanov's debriefing.

***

Hristo Boev arrived at the sports complex "Sport Palace" in the afternoon, where he met the other personal trainers of the national athletes. The national team coach Yordan Ivanov had gathered together all the mentors ten days before the European Championships, because the critical qualification trials were imminent. The composition of the team depended on the results.

"Good for you, Galabin, you are flawless," The Lizard says to Galabin as they pass each other on the stage. "Looks like Petar The Bone will lose."

"Wait and see what happens in the trials," Boevski replied with a smile.

"Are things going as planned?" Hristo Boev asks.

"Yes, Big Brother. I feel great," Galabin confirms. "The last qualification is on Friday. Yordan Ivanov wants us to do five attempts to estimate our stability."

***

"I will make just three attempts, Peter The Bone can do ten if he likes," the twenty-year-old weightlifter snapped at the national team coach Yordan Ivanov.

"As you wish. If he lifts more, you lose," the trainer

concludes.

The young man from Knezha started with the snatch and made three perfect lifts – 140, 145 and 147.5 kg. Petar "The Bone" lifted 150 kg on his fifth try and went ahead by 2.5 kg. On the second trial Petar Petrov starts with 165 kg. He lifts it. Galabin needs 170 kg for his first lift. No problem. Petar "The Bone" concludes his set at 170 kg. Boevski makes two more good lifts – 175 and 177.5 kg In total, Galabin is ahead by 5 kilos over his main competitor. Hristo Boev is happy, his nephew – twice as much. The next day Boevski will travel to Sofia, and fly to Warsaw on Sunday.

***

The phone in Knezha rings exactly at 14:30 o'clock. Hristo Boev is having a nap on a warm Sunday. At that time Galabin should have been on his way to the European Championships.

"Big Brother, they took me off the plane!" Galabin's angry voice speaks from the earpiece. "I still can't believe it."

"What?" Hristo Boev answers after five seconds delay.

"You know I've done nothing, right?" The weightlifter explains. "All they told me was that the doping test was unclear. Six more guys are like me, and two have tested positive."

"Okay, but how did this come about at two in the afternoon, just before you take off?" Hristo Boev, who usually is a calm person, exploded.

"I don't know, it was such a circus! A fight nearly broke out," Galabin adds. "I was just talking with The Lizard about how we are going to get our bonuses and finish the whole preparation off. He left, didn't get detained like me."

"Have they given you any explanation? Did they give you a piece of paper about what you are accused of?"

Hristo Boev said in a calmer voice.

"They told us it would be better if we didn't compete," Galabin laughed angrily. "You know what that means, right? I told them I would compete no matter what, and Yordan Ivanov said he wouldn't let me on the stage. They told us to keep our heads down. They were going to close their eyes and not penalize us. We could even go to the World Championships in China in the fall."

"It's clear now. They pulled a fast one on you. I would not be surprised if they swapped the samples so that someone "more prepared" can get all the medals, and you are left in the dust," Hristo Boev concluded. "You come back to Knezha now. Don't do anything foolish. We will continue training and show them who's best at a later occasion."

Hristo Boev hang up the phone and sat on the chair. He put his head in his hands and made a quick assessment of the situation. Galabin was the only boy from Knezha in the national team. Every other weightlifting school had backing – Shumen, Sliven, Sofia... Coaches and federation officials had their favourites. The people on the board of directors were arranging their boys' travel, because every medal they won meant a nice bonus not only for the weightlifter, but everyone around him also. The mayors were setting up celebrations and awards. The sponsors opened their pockets. There was no one to look after Galabin, who was supposed to lift in the seniors for the first time.

***

In the European Championships in Warsaw, Petar The Bone wins a bronze medal with a total of 310 kg. Several days earlier in the trials, Galabin made a total of 325 kg. The result is equal to that of the European champion Naim Suleymanoglu and 2.5 kg more than the second – Valerios Leonidis – a Russian, who had received Greek citizenship.

Bulgaria got only one title – Nikolay Peshalov became a European champion for the fifth time. Second was Sevdalin Minchev. Ivan Ivanov and Stefan Georgiev came home with silver and bronze in the lightest category, beaten only by Halil Mutlu – a Bulgarian, competing for Turkey. The last medal was for Plamen Bratoichev. The total was one title and five medals.

The performance was rated as a failure. The doping doubts threatened Yordan Ivanov's position, and he was replaced by the Olympic champion in Moscow '80 – the five-time World and five-time European champion Yanko Rusev.

***

Malkodanski knew Naim Suleymanoglu quite well. In 1979 Stefcho was sent to serve his military service in Kardzhali. His coach was Enver Turkileri, who created athletes like Suleymanoglu, Halil Mutlu, and Taner Sagir. At that time the future superstar Naim Suleymanoglu had the Bulgarian name of Naum Shalamanov.

The-twelve-year old boy sleeps in the same bed as Malkodanski in the army barracks, because there isn't enough room for everybody. He goes to the gym every day. Watches the others lift. Enver Turkileri does not subject him to huge lifts straight away. First, he toughens him up mentally.

"You will be Olympic champion. This is your future," the specialist explains, while everyone else in the gym wonders why Turkileri pays so much attention to the little boy.

During the World Cup in Melbourne '86, Shalamanov sides with the Turkish team and returns with them from Australia. He was only nineteen at that time, but had already won two world titles for Bulgaria. His name was changed but the golden path before him still lay ahead. He is unbeaten in every competition and breaks his own world records like tooth picks.

***

Curvaceously, long-legged German and Russian women move along Varna's central street and throw lustful looks at the strong guys drinking coffee. June's sun beats down during the day, and dusk was the time when everyone went for a walk.

"Damn, if it weren't for those camps I could have some good times here," Petar "The Bone" shakes his head. "German girls, Russian girls? No forgiveness for any of them!"

"You? All you do is drool. You probably won't get it up if it comes to it," Zlatan Vanev laughs. He is one of the athletes who had an unclear sample a few months ago, but he was called for the camp with the national team.

"Okay, Petar, how would you talk to them? You don't even speak Russian," Sevdalin Minchev says. He has already marked his place as a decent weightlifter in the seniors.

"You don't need language skills for these things, you need a hard cock!" the Bone says firmly, and causes wild laughter around the table.

"Let's go, it's getting dark. This movie has made me sleepy. You know what's waiting for us tomorrow," Boevski reminds the group.

With more jokes on the way, the company goes back to the "Sport Palace" training camp. The only one missing is Galabin's loyal friend – Stefan Georgiev. The Lizard was punished by the federation's managers for swearing at the national junior team's coach Zlatin Ivanov. Boevski's classmate furiously pursued the coach after he put the wrong weight on the bar for his final clean and jerk attempt. Georgiev finished second and swore viciously at him, for which he was removed from the team.

It was getting dark as they arrived at "Sport Palace", but the sportsmen could stay up if they wanted to. There is only one morning training on Sunday. The afternoon is the time for relaxation.

The national team's doctor is waiting for them at the door, with a sour look in his eyes.

"I won't wait for you all day to take your medicals," the grumpy doctor tries to bully the weightlifters.

"Piss off! If you don't give it today, you will tomorrow," Petar "the Bone" replies, knowing this is the first day for pills. It's not fatal, if they skip it.

The routine doping check is set for the morning. They all happily give samples, knowing they are clean.

***

"Did you take your toothbrush and your razor?" Stella asks her son, as her grandson Paul runs a toy car around his father. In the living room of the family house in Knezha the mood is excellent. Krasimira is both happy and sad, because Galabin is going away again, after being in camps for a couple of months.

"Yes, yes, I've taken everything, don't worry," the young weightlifter replies. "My bag is ready, I have enough clothes, and November is warmer in China than here."

"Daddy, Daddy, will you bring me a present?" three-year-old Paul asks.

The boy has his father's face. He has the same wide forehead and strong legs. According to Krasimira he hasn't stopped running, and breaking things with his ball. A future football talent.

"Do you want a medal?" Galabin turns with a smile towards his son. "Mother, I think I'm ready. Nothing can stop me. Hristo is also very pleased. The last trial is next, but I think it won't be a problem and I will get in the team. Come on, pour water in front of me for good luck, because I am running late."

***

Yanko Rusev already knows Galabin will be included in the squad for the World Championships in China. Boevski is in among the favourites for the 64 kg category. At 59 kg the big hopes again are on Nikolay Peshalov and Sevdalin Minchev. Bulgaria has two athletes at 70 kg – Plamen Zhelyaskov and Radostin Dimitrov. The other great star – Yoto Yotov will lift for the first time at 76 kg. He has the unique achievement of being first or second in every competition he has participated in. The young Zlatan Vanev is also in his category.

The competition is fierce, because these championships will decide the Olympic quota places. There are nearly forty athletes in a couple of categories. The biggest stars in weightlifting are ready for great battles, led by the Turks Naim Suleymanoglu and Halil Mutlu, the Greeks Leonidas Sabanis and Pyrros Dimas, and the Cuban Pablo Lara.

The strong weightlifters from the former Soviet Union are aiming for medals in every category, and the Chinese, breaking record after record, are achieving the next phenomenal results.

***

Hristo Boev is going up the stairs in the Sports Ministry. The Bulgarian Weightlifting Federation's office is there. The CEO Norair Nurikyan had invited him. He added nothing more. Boev senses there is something wrong the moment he steps into the office.

"I have bad news," the legendary weightlifter, who has two Olympic titles to his name, begins. "Galabin has been caught."

"Hey, don't mess around! How was he caught three days before the World Championships?" The coach clenches his fists.

"This is the document in English, the sample was

opened," Nurikyan gives him a piece of paper with a shaking hand.

"Where the document came from?" Hristo Boev asks. "Look, I may be a countryman, but I'm not stupid."

Nurikyan bows his head and remains silent. Years later he admitted, that at this moment he felt as if Hristo Boev would throw him out of the fourth floor window.

***

"Hey, what the hell happened?" Hristo Boev had barged into the gym of the sports complex "Dianabad", where the national team was located and shouted at the coach Yanko Rusev.

"Everything is fine, Hristo. How are you? We will destroy the Turk this year. Galabin lifted 152.5 kg and 182.5 kg," Rusev says proudly with his everlasting smile.

"How the hell are we going to defeat him, you fool? Galabin has been caught!" Hristo Boev erupts again.

"What do you mean caught?" The national team's coach honestly replies.

***

The noisiest place in the whole town was Knezha's newspaper stand. Several people had gathered, reading the headlines. The salesman could not get them to leave. Everyone shut up, when Stella Boevska approached. They made way with compassionate looks in their eyes.

She looks at the first page – "Weightlifters caught with doping before the World Championships." Her eyes focus on the article. She begins to read slowly. Her hope evaporates. The last name is Galabin's.

***

"Lizard, I am a convenient victim," Galabin shakes his head while relating what had happened. They were having coffee. "I swear to you, I haven't taken a thing. They must have switched my sample. They caught someone else. Someone who wasn't supposed to go up in flames. They tricked me again."

"You are convenient, as you and your uncle are like lone wolves," answers Stefan Georgiev. "You have no backing. You know if these things don't happen with money, they certainly do happen with a lot of money. The European Championships are one thing, the World Championships are totally different. Furthermore, it is the qualification for the Olympics in Atlanta next year."

"Everything is clear now. They wanted to get me out of the way. I could have beaten Suleymanoglu, but who am I – some peasant from Knezha. Now Abadzhiev is in Turkey. He must have had information on how much I can lift. They found out my results, and it was decided."

"You are quite right, coaches are saying the Olympic Committee is deciding on which sports to leave and which to cut. They are setting Suleymanoglu up to be the first three times Olympic champion in weightlifting. And you, who don't have a single tournament in seniors abroad, are trying to defeat him. Where are you coming from? Without a single competition abroad, you dare to challenge him! What were you thinking of?"

***

"Stefcho, tell me honestly, did you give me something?" Asked Galabin Boevski with a sharp look at his former coach.

The weightlifter was still trying to find the reason for the positive sample. He couldn't believe he had fallen prey to this.

"How could I put my own child in prison?" Malkodanski excused himself with compassion on his face. He recalled several years back, when every day he was looking after the skinny dark haired boy. The child had grown up before his eyes. Pound after pound. From one category to another. He remembered all the trials they had gone through. He recalled when they were robbed on the train to Germany, and how they played the slot machines, with money they got from a distant city's mayor, so they could save enough to return home. Memories were not helping reality.

"These things I was giving you were checked by my brother," Stefcho Malkodanski added. "You know he is a pharmacist. It is not my fault. It's coming from above. Someone is using dirty money. You were ready to defeat Suleymanoglu. That's why you were stopped."

Galabin said nothing more. He learned another life lesson. The conclusion sank into his brain and built another wall between him and the others. He felt helpless. The people who built him up as an athlete didn't have the answers to his questions. The federation's officials also couldn't say a thing. Galabin knew he would be all alone from here on.

CHAPTER IV

Krasimira was clenching little Myra's hand. She was worried, even though they were not in the prison yet. The guards were looking lustfully at the beautiful Bulgarian. They were joking in Portuguese who would be the lucky one to frisk her for metal objects. Luckily there was a woman on duty and she did the job.

The child was looking around curiously. She wondered what this place was. All she knew was that they are going to see daddy. She was impatient, but at the same time could feel her mother's anxiety. The moisture between the two hands was like a conductor for stress. Myra was clinging to her mother. She didn't want to leave her side. The kid nearly wept when the smiling unfamiliar woman searched her clothes.

Saturday morning was unusually hot for one of the coolest months of the year in Brazil. The countless doors, concrete walls and cold looks of the guards were enough to freeze the sweat on Krasimira's neck. The protocol for moving is strict. Another blue grid door is locked with a heavy padlock. It will only open, when the previous one is locked. The light from the luminescent lamps was completely absorbed by the ash-coloured walls. The only bright thing in the labyrinth was the white ceiling. Krasimira looked at it often, suffocated by claustrophobic feelings. A short Brazilian was walking in front of her. He was taking her to the meeting room. She turned to Myra. The child was walking mechanically. She was no longer turning her head around, but preferred to look forward, with her hand entangled in her mummy's.

The last door was behind them. There were a lot of people in the large room. At first Krasimira failed to get her bearings, but then she saw Galabin standing up. He walked slowly towards them and a smile shined on his face.

"Daddy, Daddy!" Myra yelled, not paying attention to the others around her. She rushed and threw herself at Galabin. He lifted and swung her around. "I love you very much"

"I love you very much too," the prisoner replied as he kissed the child's cheeks.

Krasimira relaxed. She decided to hang back, so the father and his daughter could enjoy one another. The risky trip to Brazil concealed many dangers. The last harvest had started in Knezha when they arrived. She hired a house in the town of Itai, close to the prison. It was one of the mandatory conditions when they applied for early release. The rent was high, together with bills for electricity, water and internet. The town was about 300 miles away from Sao Paulo. It had 25 000 citizens, none of them was a Bulgarian.

"Krasi, how are you? Is everything all right with the house?" Galabin took his wife away from her thoughts. Myra wasn't interested in the conversation. Instead she was trying to hug her father's thinner neck as hard as she could.

"Yes, everything is normal. Myra feels well," Krasimira answered.

This wasn't the first time she had seen her husband since he got locked up. She visited him in the second week, after he was detained. He looked despairing then. Now he knew exactly what situation he was in, and was searching for a solution with her help. Krasimira hid from him that she had started a donation account to help his release. If he found out, he would go mad, as his own pride would not let him beg. Actually this move was pointless, because no one donated.

"We already know the stores in our neighbourhood and are waiting for Sarah to arrive in two months time," Krasimira added.

"Daddy, you are coming with us, right? Mummy said you were working very far from home, and that's why you haven't come back," said the little naive girl. She had her father's almond shaped eyes and long nose.

Krasimira and Galabin looked at each other. He had no idea how his daughter remained isolated from all of the troubles. Her mother and grandmother avoided speaking about her daddy's whereabouts when she was around. However, the child had found out in her own way. When she saw bars in a cartoon she would say, "This is a prison, I don't want to look at it."

"Myra," Galabin said slowly to his youngest child, while looking into her eyes. "I am not working, my girl. This is a prison. And I can't leave."

***

The Bulgarian Weightlifting Federation's Executive Board had gathered. The first order of business was the national team's performance at the World Championships in China '95. The primary task was complete. The weightlifters had won a full set of Olympic quotas for Atlanta '96. Everything else was a failure – only two medals. Yoto Yotov got the silver, and Nikolay Peshalov won bronze. In the most dramatic category – 64 kg, Naim Suleymanoglu and Valerios Leonidis tied, with a total of 327.5 kg, but the Turk of Bulgarian heritage won his fifth world title due to his lighter weight.

The last item on the agenda was the fate of Galabin Boevski. He received a two-year sentence for doping.

No one remembered, that just a few days before the World Championships the talented sportsman from Knezha scored 335 kg in training, which would have granted him the gold medal and victory over the great Naim Suleymanoglu.

***

"You should not stop, Galabin, because if you do, it will be very difficult to stay within the category, and the burden of the barbell will be greater," Hristo Boev said.

The trainer and athlete were sitting together in his uncle's house. They knew it would come to this conversation. The young weightlifter had lost everything. A decade of hard work was gone.

"Two years is a long time, Big Brother," Boevski replied, and from his tone Hristo sensed he had not forgotten the way he was framed for doping. "Krasi is pregnant again. Paul is growing, and look what's happening in the country. Half of Knezha has become unemployed."

"I have friends here and there, I will try to arrange something. Meanwhile, you have to come to the gym and keep in shape," the coach continued. "I know you are working as a security guard and controlling the slot machines in Knezha. This is not for you. You are an athlete."

***

The last big competition before the Olympics in Atlanta '96 was the European Championships in the city of Stavanger, Norway. Half of the team was from Galabin's generation. Zlatan Vanev won his first European title in seniors. The Lizard finished second. He had no luck, because the unbeatable Halil Mutlu was lifting in his category. After this competition The Turkish star didn't lose a single championship in the next twelve years. During that time he won three Olympic, four World, and eight European titles. Sevdalin Minchev, Petar "The Bone" and Plamen Zhelyazkov also came back with silver medals. Ilian Iliev and Plamen Bratoychev added bronze medals.

During that time Hristo Boev kept to his word. Boevski was keeping out of trouble and worked as a chauffeur for a local businessman. The boss was understanding towards the weightlifter's desire to train, and was letting him go any chance he had.

In the mornings Galabin was waiting for his employer and then driving around with him. Sitting still behind the wheel and long hours of waiting were boring for him. He missed the crash of the weights on the floor on the stage. The steady bouncing was sounding through his head. For the first time in his life he felt nostalgia for the constant muscle pain he used to feel after training.

***

The TV in Knezha was on all night. Galabin was crossing his fingers for his teammates and imagined himself lifting on the most prestigious of stages. The coach Yanko Rusev took ten weightlifters to the Olympics in Atlanta.

In the first category, Sevdalin Minchev won a medal. He was in the lightest division and after five successful attempts climbed onto the winners' rostrum. The second medal came from Nikolay Peshalov (59 kg), who was close to scoring zero in the clean and jerk, after two unsuccessful attempts. He got the barbell right on his third. In Galabin's category Ilian Iliev and Petar "The Bone" remained sixth and ninth. The title was won by Naim Suleymanoglu with a total of 335 kg Boevski had lifted the same weight nine months earlier in training.

A few weeks after the Olympics, the family's house in Knezha begun to feel small. Galabin and Krasi's second child – Sarah first saw the light of day on the 2nd of December, 1996. The daughter was named after the first letter of her grandmother Stella's name.

**

"Mother, I am leaving for Sofia," Galabin said firmly one spring day. The crisis in Bulgaria was at its peak. Several months earlier Jan Videnov's government had fallen, but that didn't seem to help. The hunger of January[11] continued into February, March, April... The electricity bills were as high as a month's salary. "I am the head of a family now. I have responsibilities as a husband and a parent."

Boevski looked determined. Energy was radiating from his face, and the decision was already made.

"Is there someone to take you? You don't think it's better there than here, do you? Don't forget you will have to pay rent. Who will look after the children if they get sick, and you are out working?" The mother of the weightlifter tried her last ploy.

"Krasimira can manage," Galabin looked at his wife. "She won't work. I have already talked with my Olympic Hopes' trainer Tzviatko Petkov. He has a club right next to the Dianabad' weightlifting complex. He will take me to work there during the night. In the day I will train and try to get back into the national team."

---

[11] The hunger of January 1997 was the most difficult period of time for Bulgaria since the fall of Communism. Rampant inflation brought people out onto the streets and they brought down the government of Jan Videnov. The national currency, the lev, lost thousand times its value within a few months.

***

Just a few days before the fall of Jan Videnov's government, the legendary coach Ivan Abadzhiev returned to Bulgaria. The specialist from the town of Novi Pazar started his career as a coach in 1969. He implemented a unique methodology of training, based on brutal weights. It wasn't long before it gave results, and Bulgaria became a leading force in world weightlifting.

Abadzhiev's halo was dispelled during the Olympics in Seoul '88. The champions Mitko Grablev and Angel Genchev were caught with a forbidden substance, a banned diuretic. Their medals were taken from them. The rest of Bulgarian team, represented by the superstars in world weightlifting – Asen Zlatev, Rumen Teodosiev, Ivan Chakarov, Stefan Botev and Antonio Krastev, were disqualified.

Abadzhiev left the national team. He was elected as representative for the Grand National Assembly, but resigned soon after. In the middle of the nineties he took on Turkey's team and became famous in the Olympics in Atlanta with the titles of Halil Mutlu and Naim Suleymanoglu. Jealousy of his success cost him his position. The Turkish coaches and athletes started a rebellion. They didn't want to train with his harsh procedures. They were afraid they might cripple themselves if they followed all the instructions given by Abadzhiata.

***

"If someone wants to train, I'll open the gym. The barbells are there, the platforms too. There won't be any money, because you can see for yourself the state of our country," Abadzhiev's words flowed slowly, as he gazed at the athletes with his typical sad look.

A dozen of Bulgaria's top weightlifters were in the gym. Some of their colleagues had already figured out that they could make no money in sports. It was a lot easier to sell their strong bodies to criminal groups, shaking the last pennies from the poor.

"I'm off." Says two-time World junior champion Ilian Tsankov, who gets up and leaves. The promising Marin Shikov, who is undisputed World and European champion in the juniors, follows.

***

Hotel "Diana 1" was frozen on the outside as well as the inside. The weightlifters from the national team were shivering like dogs. The rickety wooden framing on the windows was making strange noises in the wind.

"I've been all over the world, and haven't seen a more miserable hotel than this one," The Lizard crosses himself.

"Come on, Zlatan, get out of that bathroom! Three more are waiting," the bronze medalist from the Olympics in Atlanta Sevdalin Minchev shouts out.

"Guys, do you think we can get four people for a round of belote?" Asks the rookie Georgi Gardev from the city of Pazardzhik, who was a European champion in juniors and is now in his first year in seniors.

"That would be difficult. And belote makes you hungry very fast. Abadzhiev promised to find something to eat, because they have stopped all funds from the sports committee," Stefan Georgiev says firmly.

***

"There will be salami, no problem," the newly elected president of the Weightlifting Federation, Orlin Rizov shouts. The businessman and a representative was all red. Obviously he had been drinking the whole night. He entered the room as an old official. The weightlifters looked at each other. They expected more. Their salaries were 10 000 levs, which at that time was equal to 15 dollars.

Abadzhiata was pleased. Rizov arrived with three huge beef salamis, a meter and a half long and extremely thick. The weightlifters laughed their hats off when they saw them. The Olympic champion from Moscow '80 Asen Zlatev also helped. He had a dairy farm and was regularly bringing in big cheese tins. All the products were kept in a huge refrigerator. Two prospective soldiers, hired by the Senior Trainer and sleeping in the coach's room, were taking care of the food. Before the end of the morning training the soldiers were cooking the lunch. They were cutting the salami into round pieces that could feed five men each.

Olga, the manager of the hotel, was letting the rookie chefs throw the salami on the grill. The whole scheme was Abadzhiev's idea. The goal was to save some money from food, so he could take as many athletes to camp as possible.

"There will be salami and there will be cheese," the weightlifters were imitating the federation's president and looking at the rookies added, "You can have it raw or grilled, if you like"

"What salamis, what rubbish? My goal is to go to World and European Championships and fulfill my dream. I've come this far, I'm not giving up," Georgi Gardev was naively thinking, as he munched on the giant "Kamchia" salami.

***

Soon after the police investigator left the gym, Ivan Abadzhiev went mad. They had just a few days before the World Junior Championships in Cape Town. The Senior Trainer will only send two athletes – Georgi Markov from Bourgas, who won the European title in the juniors last year, and the heavyweight Damian Damianov.

"Are you guys crazy?" Abadzhiev turns to the two national athletes. "What are these fights all about? You stained the walls of the rooms with champagne. Are you animals or athletes? I'm done with you. You will travel, because we can't refund the tickets and reservations, but you are off the national team afterwards."

Markov and Damianov are in great shape. They both come back with gold medals and are met with flowers and hugs at the airport. From Abadzhiev they receive the news, that despite their success, they have been expelled from the national team.

***

At his first competition in the seniors, after his return to the national team, Ivan Abadzhiev creates a furore. Bulgaria wins two titles in the European Championships in Rijeka (Croatia) – by Nikolay Peshalov and Yoto Yotov. Sevdalin Minchev and Zlatan Vanev finish with silver, and Stefan Georgiev and Plamen Zhelyazkov return with bronze medals. The debutant Georgi Gardev competes with dignity and finishes fourth.

The night after the end of the championship Nikolay Peshalov is invited into the club of local weightlifting legends. The gold medalist receives a tempting offer to lift for Croatia. His monthly salary would be equal to his yearly one in Bulgaria. The bonuses for a gold medal from a major competition would be many times bigger. Peshalov proves himself worth it and wins the Olympic title for his second country in Sydney, three years later.

***

The success in Rijeka echoes like a bell in the weightlifting community. Abadzhiata's magic brings back more weightlifters who had run away when the money was short.

Training days consist of two sessions. On Monday, Wednesday and Friday there are three practice sessions a day. The trial tests are on those days. The goal of the weightlifters is to lift the maximum they are capable of, as the numbers are going into the head coach book. After the trials there was another evening training. The exhausted weightlifters are required to lift 5 or 7.5 kilograms less than the maximum they got at the last training session. If they could not do it, Abadzhiev was certain – they had cheated on the weights. The participants for the World and European Championships are taken from these qualification sessions.

In the morning, the first practice session starts at 9 am and ends in 1 pm. The second is from 4 pm to 7.30 pm. If there is a third it starts after dinner and goes on until 11 pm. Sometimes the weightlifters stay up until midnight, because Abadzhiata likes to make an in depth analysis.

***

Every evening Galabin starts his shift at the disco club "Strong 205", which is 100 metres away from the national team's gym of "Dianabad". The club is owned by his former coach from "Olympic Hopes", Tzviatko Petkov. The number in the name comes from the maximum weight the owner was able to lift, when he was an athlete.

In the days when there is no work, Boevski finds other places to make money. He looks small, and doesn't get the drunken customers' respect, but he can count on his strong thighs if needed. The job is sometimes dirty, but at home Sarah needs nappies and naughty Paul is starting school in a couple of years.

***

"Hey Galabin, where have you been?" Stefan Georgiev meets his classmate with a sturdy handshake. "How's work? Are you holding up?"

"It's not for me," the weightlifter from Knezha admits, as he has also put on a couple of pounds. Boevski has some time before starting his shift and decides to see his old friends at the national team's training gym. "I deal with drunkards all night long. Tell me how is training going with Abadzhiev?"

"I won't lie to you, it's very tough. He is tearing us apart. Everything in my body hurts, but it's worth it, because we get results," the Lizard replies, while putting 25 kg weights on the barbell.

"It would be nice, if we had a masseuse," the voice of Georgi Gardev is heard. "Other sports, where training is easier, use masseuses, but we don't."

The rookies' words are heard by the ever-vigilant Ivan Abadzhiev. The Senior Trainer moves forward. All eyes are on him.

"Gardev, tell me, when Kumcho Valcho chased Zayo Bayo[12], Zayo Bayo yelled out: Kumcho Valcho wait a bit so I can get a massage, and then you can chase me then?" Calmly and sparingly he parried the request for a masseuse. "You have to be ready for extremes. Galabin, I've heard of you. You had great results as a youngster. If you want to try out, come on in, the gym is open. I can take you to camp, if you can achieve the standard. You have time, because your penalty expires at the end of the year. When you are ready, come along."

---

[12] Kumcho Valcho and Zayo Bayo are heroes from Bulgarian fairy tales. The former is a wolf, the latter a rabbit

CHAPTER V

The thumb and forefinger were driving the thread on confidently. The green cloth was just about enough for the job. The second bracelet was ready. Galabin returned to reality. He no longer paid attention to the colourless walls. The mandatory white shirt for all "guests" of the Itai Prison was too big for him until a couple of months ago. He hadn't started push ups and the other exercises back then. The kilograms lost after his arrest at the airport were put back on. Now the beige prison trousers were stretched.

"They must have picked this colour because the dirt doesn't show," the Bulgarian thought, looking at every prisoner in the room. They were all dressed in white shirts and beige pants.

White, green and red. Finally something colourful in this blue-grey hole. The colours of the Bulgarian flag, for the honour of which Galabin lifted all those years, were now on the bracelets, braided by him personally in the prison's workshop. The place was always full, because every criminal could reduce his sentence there. For three workdays the prisoners received one day bonus, which was set against the time spent in the jail. This didn't apply to him, because, he didn't have a sentence yet.

The beautiful bracelets were for Paul and Sarah. Braiding the symbolical threads on the Bulgarian flag the weightlifter raised at the World and European Championships, he missed a large part of their childhood. Month after month in camps, year after year in competitions. The endless rollercoaster of his sporting life cost him those most precious moments.

He recalled his colleagues in the national team receiving news of the birth of their children on the phone. They could not even bring them into the municipality. They waited for the competition to end, then had a day or two off, before the wheel spun again.

"Was it all worth it?" Galabin asked himself, clenching the newly made bracelets.

***

"Bulgaria wins third title in the World Championships in Chiang Mai (Thailand). Yoto Yotov put on the gold medal in the 76 kg division with a total of 367.5 kg," rang out the happy voice of journalist Teodor Chereshev on the radio, during the sports news on the "Horizon" station. "Second was another of our athletes, Georgi Gardev, with a total of 365 kg. These were the last two Bulgarians in the championships. The national team had great success in the competition. Other gold medals were won by Stefan Georgiev at 59 kg and Zlatan Vanev at 70 kg. Sevdalin Minchev took the bronze, and the other two national weightlifters – Naiden Rusev and Valentin Sarov finished fourth. This was the first World Championships, in which our national team was headed by Ivan Abadzhiev, after his return at the beginning of the year."

Galabin felt the kitchen close in on him after he heard the good news. The adrenalin began to flow. He could feel his hands shaking from desire to grasp the barbell. The evening training was an hour away. He had decided. He would spend extra time in the gym. He wanted to use every minute to chase the norms Abadzhiev had set for him.

Sarah cried in the next room. Paul yelled. Krasimira scolded the kid. The children were growing, and money was short. He reached into his pockets. It would have been better if he didn't. He wondered how they would survive if he started training twice a day.

***

"The Chinese was very tough. Nothing was certain until the end, but I was 400 grams lighter than him," The Lizard tells his classmate the incredible drama in the World Championships in Thailand. Galabin is listening with interest and a little bit of jealousy. "My heart was going to pop out as I was looking at him, trying to lift 167.5 kg on his last attempt. If he had lifted it, I would have been second. I jumped like Michel Jordan when he dropped it."

"It was about time for you, after all those second and third places you had," Galabin said. "I have made my decision to come back. My ban expires in two months. I am training hard, but I have to work, and that stands in my way," he admits honestly, as he revolves his cigarette between his fingers. "I take every shift I can get, and the money is always short. I don't know what to do anymore."

***

Galabin is speaking on the phone with Hristo Boev a couple of times a week. He carefully writes down his trainer's instructions. Boevski exercises strictly and respects Knezha's weightlifting school. Training is once a day, but there is nothing unnecessary in it. This works out well for Galabin, because he doesn't have time for two training sessions a day. The results are coming slowly but surely. Abadzhiev's norms now look completely attainable after two years away. The talented sportsman from Knezha is ready to be tested in the European Championships in April, 1998.

***

Zlatan Vanev completes his fifth successful attempt. He has a total of 360 kg, which wins him the European title. The audience in Riesa (Germany) begins to clap. The weightlifter from Shumen rotates his shoulders, and stretches his neck, ready to go again. The incredible weight of 205.5 kg lights up on the board – a new world record in the clean and jerk.

Abadzhiata encourages Zlatan on his way. Vanev has lifted heavier weights in training. He knows the competition has begun in the best possible way. He grasps the barbell and does the move mechanically. Something happens. It is like his left arm is falling. The barbell drops. A muffled groan fills the hall. A piercing cry rings around the stage, because his elbow has been dislocated.

***

The TV is showing a replay of the serious injury. It was as if thunder and lightning had struck on the Boevski house in Knezha. Stella has covered her face with her hands. Her eyes are wet with tears. She knows her son is set to return to the sport. He is about to get back under the heavy barbell, where anything could happen. She looks at the phone, recites the things she would say to him in her mind.

"I should not call," Stella Boevski thinks. "I would put negative things in his mind. He is heading for the top, and I must not stop him."

***

Abadzhiev goes on with his success. The Bulgarians are team champions after they win the titles in the first four categories in the European Championships in Riesa. Ivan Ivanov, Stefan Georgiev, Plamen Zhelyazkov and Zlatan Vanev in plaster return home with gold. Ivan Chakarov is second, Naiden Rusev is third. Georgi Gardev finishes fourth.

There is wild celebration. The newspapers are bursting with praise for Bulgarian weightlifting. The journalists recount there are only two years to the Olympics in Sydney.

***

The weightlifter from Knezha opens the door of the room without having the screeching, typical of the "Diana 1" Hotel. After the national team's success at the World Championships in 1997 and the four titles from the European Championships in Riesa in 1998, a lot of things have changed. In times of crisis all other Bulgarian sports have failed. Only the weightlifters return with a basket full of medals. The businessmen open their pockets, and the national athletes move to the refurbished "Diana 3" Hotel. "Overgaz" and the Combine for non-ferrous metals become sponsors of the federation. Bulgarian emigrants in Germany help with money and send a full set of equipment to the weightlifters.

The room Galabin enters has two beds. Georgi Gardev lies on one of them. The weightlifters know each other from the years they spent together in the junior team of Ivan Lechev.

"Listen, I'm going to tell you something, but if I hear my words from another mouth, I won't speak to you anymore," the talented sportsman from Knezha begins, not so diplomatically, as he sits on his bed.

"If that's what you think of me, you can just get up and leave," Gardev replies. He looks more like a drummer than a weightlifter with his curly hair. "How will I know you haven't told anyone else? I don't want to hear anything about it."

"I haven't and I will tell you," Galabin answers preoccupied. He is two years older than his roommate. "This training Abadzhiev is putting us through is not really right. I will keep to the training programme of my coach Hristo Boev."

Just before he got into the national team, Boevski received instructions from his mentor. He is not to show how he is getting on with the large weights he is lifting. Instead, he would steadily increase his weights by 2.5 kilograms every few days.

"This way you will please Abadzhiev, and won't overtrain yourself with his system. You will increase your weights using our plan," cunning Hristo Boev told him.

***

Plamen Asparuhov is sitting at the bar of the disco club "Strong 205". He refused the whisky offered by the bartender. He came here with an agenda. His club "Ladimex" from the miners' town of Pernik is home to the best Bulgarian weightlifters. Their sponsor is the local businessman Lucy Stoykov, who made a fortune in scrap metal trading. The rich man is owner of the fashion agency "Ivet Fashion", and is rumored in the criminal community, to be the representative of the mafia organization "VIS – 2" for Pernik.

"Join us, you will have a salary, peace of mind and able to think only of training," Plamen Asparuhov dangles the bait. "We will pay your rent, and all we want from you to win medals."

"I don't know," Boevski replies. His competition rights have been restored. "I have a duty to my uncle Hristo

Boev. He was with me in my darkest moments. Let me think about it."

***

"What should I do, Big Brother?" Galabin asks his relative face to face. "It's not fair to you, if I go to Pernik. We dreamed of titles and medals together."

"You should go," the coach says firmly. "I will continue helping you with whatever you need! I can't give you a salary to lift for our club in Knezha. You have children. Don't worry about me."

Galabin's state of affairs is very bad. There are days when the money in his pocket is only enough for a pack of cigarettes. He gives everything else to Krasimira, so the kids are well-fed and dressed.

***

"I'll tell you how it will work out," Stefan Georgiev begins. "You will come to Pernik with us for the party to honour the European title. We will get together in a restaurant. You are a friend of mine, we'll have a shot of rakia, you will meet him, and it will work out. You do know Plamen Asparuhov wants you, right?"

"What party? Do you imagine Abadzhiev letting us go?" Galabin replies, as he spits a thin stream of saliva between his teeth onto the ground.

"Relax, I have already asked him. We finish our training, get in the car at four, and arrive in Pernik by five for the evening practice. We will be in the restaurant by eight, and get back in the evening and train in the morning. It's all set."

"I don't know, I don't want to have a conversation around a party table. It's not very professional," Galabin tries to refuse. "I want us to have a serious conversation, my future depends on it."

"Don't worry," The Lizard continues, feeling Galabin's defences cracking. "We will have a good time, and Ludmil Stoykov will be in a good mood. Plamen knows how to work him."

***

The band was playing "Radka the pirate" and "Tiger, Tiger"[13] over and over again. The glasses were overfilled, and the hot grilled meat on the table was banishing any thought of watching their weight. The European champion Stefan Georgiev was in the middle. Ludmil Stoykov was sitting at his side, and Boevski was nervously fidgeting on the other. Plamen Asparuhov and Yoto Yotov faced them.

The rich man was happy. His boys had taken two world titles and one European title during the year.

"Hey boss, this is the guy I'm arranging to get. He is top-notch, I tell you. He is ready for an Olympic medal," Plamen Asparuhov turns on his charming voice.

"It is decided – take him!" says the sports benefactor Lucy Stoykov without thinking.

***

The last workout in Pernik was at its peak. The big star Yoto Yotov was feeling at home. On the neighbouring stages Galabin Boevski and Damian Damianov, who was removed from the national team, were getting ready. The heavyweight division talent still hadn't forgiven Abadzhiev for his expulsion.

---

[13] "Radka the pirate" and "Tiger, tiger" – legendary folklore music hits in Bulgaria, during the '90s.

"You have to be very careful with the Senior Trainer. If he doesn't like you, you will have trouble," bald headed Damianov says. He talks slowly, and his words are full of hate. "You will see for yourself his system is not the best. The coaches say in the old days he had 7-8 men in every division. The choice was wide. It was a massacre. He didn't care if you damaged yourself, because there were others waiting. If you got injured, he wouldn't even remember your name. He is doing the same thing now, and we are ten men in the team.

"I will train using my personal trainer Hristo Boev's procedures. We had the best results that way," Galabin agrees, because he had heard what the training sessions were like under Abadzhiev.

"I hear he is preparing Georgi Markov for your category. He is very strong," Damianov added.

"Even better for both of us. We will compete with each other," Boevski said happily, as he was afraid of no man.

"You are smart to keep away from the thugs during your ban. It's a lot more complicated now for me. You can see they don't want me in the national team. I don't know what is going to happen, but I have to earn cash some way," added the World junior champion.

"Things are better now in the club. It is very important for an athlete not to have to worry what his wife and children are going to eat," Boevski, whose results were stabilizing daily, confirmed. "I feel sad when I start going to camps, and don't see Paul and Sarah. It's a complete pain to keep us isolated for so long."

"It's a pain for you, but essential for the likes of me, so we don't get distracted," said Damian Damianov, who was not one of the strictest regime followers among the elite weightlifters.

***

Abadzhiev had gathered the national athletes for a camp before the World Championships in Lahti (Finland). Four years after the European Championships for juniors in Rome, Galabin had a chance to set foot on an international stage. This would be the second big competition, after the European championships in Riesa, in which the men's categories would be cut back. It would be 8, down from 10.

Galabin doesn't have much of choice. His previous category – 64 kg, no longer existed. He had gained some weight and it is clear there is no way he could compete in 62 kg, where Sevdalin Minchev had an almost reserved place in the squad. His goal was 69 kg, where Plamen Zhelyazkov had established his position.

About twenty weightlifters are competing for eight positions in the national team. The battle would be tough.

***

The knock on the door was followed by a calm "Get up". Ivan Abadzhiev was the only coach in the world to personally wake his weightlifters. Galabin got up and reached for the pack of "Victory"[14]. The window was wet with condensation during the night, and outside the dirty Sofia mist was obscuring everything. On the second knock Gardev jumped up and opened the window.

"Georgi, shut it, we will catch a cold!" Boevski breathed out.

"Galab, if you don't throw away that cigarette, I won't close it," grumpily Gardev replied, using the short form of Galabin's name.

"Oh come on, why are you pretending to be a non-

---

[14] "Victory" a popular brand of cigarettes.

smoker?" Galabin said as he put on the national team's tracksuit.

"Am I smoking – yes, I am, but I never light a cigarette before noon," the weightlifter from Pazardzhik sniffed and headed for the bathroom. At least there the air wasn't smoky.

"Here, I give you my word – if I become an Olympic champion, I will stop smoking," Boevski vowed.

"Ha ha ha," Gardev laughed and even splattered the mirror with toothpaste. "It would be easier for you to become an Olympic champion than quit smoking."

Ivan Abadzhiev didn't cause trouble over smoking. All athletes knew it was not healthy for them. The bad habit had a serious effect on football players, boxers, athletes and cyclists who used their lungs more. For weightlifters smoking was harmless, and most of the athletes in the national team always had a stash of cigarettes.

Galabin tried smoking for the first time in "Olympic Hopes". It was just showing off at first. Ten boys gathered money together for a box, which emptied quite fast. The talented sportsman from Knezha started smoking seriously after the doping scandal in 1995.

***

Galabin was lifting hard during training. Things were working out. After each session Boevski went back to the room and opened a lined notebook. He marked his progress and kept everything according to plan.

In the evenings the weightlifter, who would turn 24 in a month, called his uncle. He gave an account of his progress. They were discussing the problems on the technical side. Galabin was pleased with the progress he had made. Abadzhiev too. The Senior Trainer decided to trust Boevski who officially became part of the national team's squad.

***

On one of the last training sessions prior to leaving for Finland Galabin put a wet shirt on his back. He was warm and didn't feel the cold seeping into his back. The pain came on steadily. Two days before the competition his shoulder blade was hurting badly. The doctor was helpless. He explained the muscles contracted faster due to the sudden change in temperature. The pain was coming from a pinched nerve. The trauma could be healed in a couple of days, if treated correctly, but at its peak it made the body very sore.

"Doctor, I feel like a cane, what should I do?" Galabin, worried, asked on the day of his competition. He knew Abadzhiev didn't accept injury as an excuse for failure. If he had to, the Senior Trainer would let a weightlifter compete with one arm.

"The injection would not help a lot," the national team's doctor replied. "Bear in mind, that when the barbell presses down on you, you will have trouble breathing."

Galabin returned to weightlifting competitions in 1998

***

The usual suspects for the titles Halil Mutlu and Leonidas Sabanis became champions. In the previous two days Ivan Ivanov and Sevdalin Minchev won the bronze medals in the 56 and 62 kilograms divisions. The Greek nearly lost the gold. The Croatian debutant Nikolay Peshalov made two unsuccessful attempts, which would have put him at the top.

Galabin started with his regular weight of 152.5 kg. He lifted it successfully. The other Bulgarian in this category Plamen Zhelyazkov began with an excellent attempt at 155 kg. Boevski continued with 157.5 but failed twice. His teammate went ahead with 160 kg – a new world record. In the second part of the competition Galabin succeeded in lifting only the starting weight of 185 kg, which sent him down to fourth place. The title went to Zhelyazkov with another world record of 350 kg in the total.

In the next category – 77 kg, Zlatan Vanev had miraculously recovered from the elbow dislocation seven months ago. He won the gold medal and Petar Tanev finished second.

Galabin's roommate Georgi Gardev finished fifth. He had the chance to take the bronze, but failed twice in attempts with the required weight.

***

On his return from Lahti, Ivan Abadzhiev was again the centre of attention due to the world titles. The media had not forgotten the doping scandal in the Olympics at Seoul '88.

"There are no longer athletes who become champions without taking drugs," the Senior Trainer says to journalists. "Doping is a relative thing. If a drug is not on the forbidden list today, it will be tomorrow. My desire is for all athletes to use only vitamins."

It was said that Abadzhiev was going to slaughterhouses to collect oxen testicles, so his weightlifters could get stronger. With or without it, this was the second year that Bulgarian athletes earned respect.

"It occurred to me that the International Federation's president isn't so happy when he kisses our champions, as opposed to the moments when he was awarding Halil Mutlu and Leonidas Sabanis their titles. This shows they are afraid of Bulgarian weightlifting again," Abadzhiev adds in his interviews.

***

Galabin wasn't happy with his fourth place. First he looked for the cause in himself. The injury wasn't an excuse. He felt there was something else.

"I lost so much in those years of inaction," he said to himself. Plamen Asparuhov was sitting in front of him, trying to cheer up his athlete. "I lack routine. The feeling for stage and barbell is missing. I am trying to isolate myself from the audience, with its noises, the camera lights and flashes."

"I know what you need," Plamen Asparuhov, who everyone called "Feefee the Feather" ever since his athlete years, said slowly. "I will set you up to lift in Germany. They wanted Georgi Markov, but you will go instead."

***

The season in the German Bundesliga is from the end of September until March. It has 8-9 competitions a year. Boevski was attracted by the club "Soest". Abadzhiev didn't approve of this practice, because he was losing control over the national athletes, but there was no way to stop it, due to the excellent pay. Galabin was travelling on Friday, and coming back on Sunday. For every trip he was paid 4000 deutschmarks, to which were added bonuses for good performance.

Working abroad was welcomed for Galabin. With the money he stabilized his finances and achieved something else. Time was slipping by, and his sporting life wasn't going to last forever. Galabin thought over his past, and realized he had lost long years which he could have spent improving himself. His good friend Georgi Gardev helped him. The two of them were learning about 15-20 German words each evening. They practised in the shops. Gardev knew more, because he had been lifting in the local championship since 1995, and Boevski started at the end of 1998.

***

"You always had problems doing a lot of successful attempts in a championship," The Lizard said, analysing his former roommate's problems. The two of them were sitting in the same café as when they had decided to go to Lucy Stoykov's banquet last season. "Look at the way you learned not to make mistakes. You were ready for world records when you were in the juniors, but still remained third and fourth."

"Good point," Boevski admitted, looking through the window. Out there the snowflakes were being tossed in the powerful wind and floated away from the ground. "I used to do three successful attempts, and now I am a lot more stable with five or six. I don't have wide variations in kilograms, 2.5 the most in each competition. Things are starting to work out."

Galabin understood the change. While they were talking, his thoughts were busy with something else. For the first time in a couple of years he had enough money for the Christmas presents Paul and Sarah wanted.

CHAPTER VI

The sun was setting slowly above the prison courtyard. There was still time before it sank under the bars. Until then, Galabin would be in his cell. The well-known routine repeated itself for a whole year.

Another week passed. Time that left no memories. But this week the weightlifter would remember forever. One hour ago Krasimira and Myra left after the Sunday visit. The news they brought shook him.

Galabin smiled bitterly. He remembered all those stories, which began with the words "Do you want the good news first, or the bad?" The balance was bit different this time. One was good, the other two – bad.

He knew the good one was on its way a long time ago – Paul's baby was born. A son, who would carry the name Galabin.

The bad news was that the second court hearing had confirmed the sentence of nine years and four months. That was enough to make him furious. The damned Brazilian justice system was working in a strange way.

The last news crushed him. He didn't want to believe it, but the inevitable had happened. His father Peppy had passed away after three years battling against cancer of the lymph nodes. Galabin did everything he could. He used his connections with close and not so close people. They experimented with chemical and x-ray treatments. He didn't give up until the end.

"Dad, there are people who have been cured. Believe!" the son told to his father after every unsuccessful attempt to beat the tumor. The pain of losing a parent was hard for Galabin to bear. The unsaid words between them froze on their lips.

"I could not even bury my father," the Olympic, World and European champion bowed his head. No one saw if a tear fall from the eyes of the former Bulgarian hero.

***

"Galab, you are swinging back a little bit during the lift," Georgi Gardev said abruptly as he sat on the bench.

A second ago Boevski had made another attempt with the barbell in "Dianabad" gym. The two of them had an agreement to help each other and get rid of their technical mistakes. They were lifting on same stage. When one of them rested, the other observed. After that they analysed the situation.

"Oh, come on, Georgi, I'm doing everything right. I am motivated, tuned up and you…" Galabin goes mad and looks at Gardev with blood red eyes.

The next moment he realized his friend had not done anything wrong. Boevski wasn't able to make a correction, because he was obliged to raise a heavier weight with each successful lift. That was Abadzhiev's system. It didn't include analysis of the technical posture of the legs, back, and shoulders. Galabin was lucky he had someone to help him.

***

In pre-Olympic 1999 all the stars set out their stall. The Spanish city of La Coruna gathered the elite to battle for the European title. The Olympic silver medalist Valerios Leonidis was aiming for the gold in the 69 kg division, but it was clear from his first lifts that he would finish far behind the two Bulgarians. The Greek scored 150 kg in the snatch. Boevski started at this weight and finished successfully at 160 kg. After him in second place was the champion from last year Plamen Zhelyazkov with 157 kg.

The battle continued until the last, sixth attempt. Both national athletes lifted consecutively 182.5, 187.5 and 192.5 kg in the clean and jerk. Galabin became champion with 352.5 kg in total and Zhelyazkov took the silver with 2.5 kilograms less.

The boy from Knezha had made six successful attempts, leaving no chance for his opponents.

The night before the competition Abadzhiev announces to the media his team is not in optimal form. Despite that the national athletes win two more titles – Sevdalin Minchev and Petar Tanev. Georgi Markov and Georgi Gardev get the silver medal, while Ivan Ivanov finishes with bronze. Bulgaria is team champion.

"Mister Abadzhiev, you didn't believe we would perform so well," the journalists discuss the success with the Senior Trainer. "Did you expect such a strong performance from Galabin Boevski?

"We must wait to see the doping test and then we'll talk," Abadzhiev replies off the record. The coach's words appear in the Bulgarian newspapers, exposing for the first time the tension between Knezha's weightlifter and the legendary specialist.

***

The weightlifting gym is in high spirits. The competition is very tough. Fifteen elite athletes are preparing for the World Championships in Athens, the most important competition in the last three years, because Olympic quotas are won with it. Ivan Abadzhiev sees the desire of all athletes, but there are only eight positions in the squad. The wily coach finds a solution. He starts negotiations with the new Federation of Qatar. The mediator is the track-and-field coach Yanko Bratoev. Abadzhiata decides to send eight men to the Arab country, so they can participate on its behalf in the World Championships. The plan is clever, because the motivation of his team stays high.

The Bulgarian Federation receives 40 000 USD a year from those transfers. The salaries of the new Qatari athletes are 800 dollars. The weightlifters keep 500. The rest go to the Federation, according to the contract. Apart from that, Bulgaria receives 50% of the bonuses of the athletes, promised to them for success in major competitions.

The coach would be Abadzhiev's assistant – Zlatin Ivanov. The oil giant quickly issues passports to the Bulgarians. Among them are the European champion Petar Tanev (77 kg) and Boevski's former partner in the school escapades at "Olympic Hopes" – Yani Marchokov (105 kg). They receive new names – Badr Salem and Jaber Saeed Salem.

***

"This cannot go on!" Plamen Zhelyazkov shouts at the meeting organized by his colleagues from the national team and in the presence of Ivan Abadzhiev. "We are wrecking ourselves for pathetic salaries. The Greeks receive ten times more than us. The Turks as well. Are we the poorest country in the world?"

"You cannot stop us from competing for our clubs abroad, because we don't get paid enough here. If you don't let us go we will no longer continue to lift for the national team," Galabin Boevski adds.

His words are addressed at the Senior Trainer, who is openly opposed to his athletes' practice of working abroad.

Abadzhiev is not happy at losing control over his weightlifters before the Olympics. Furthermore, they often return with injuries and in bad shape from competitions in Germany, Italy and Netherlands.

"There is no point in setting up a boycott," Ivan Abadzhiev tries to defuse the tension. "You grew too proud of the results we achieved. If you want me gone, launch a petition. I will leave you in peace if you don't want me."

Weighty words were spoken at last. The Federation was trying to find money. The sponsors were keeping their pockets zipped up, and the Ministry of Sport didn't have the funds needed to provide the conditions desired by Abadzhiev.

***

Leaving the gym after another successful tournament in the German Bundesliga, Galabin sees one of his club officials getting into a Volkswagen Golf II. He goes to the window and speaks to him in his improved German. Boevski understands the car has been manufactured in 1991.

The owner, happy in the interest shown, invites the local club's star out for a spin. Knezha's weightlifter doesn't wait for a second invitation. He takes a comfortable seat, reaches for the gear stick and notices that the car is automatic. Boevski enjoys driving it. He is delighted. The vehicle is stable and big enough for him, Krasimira, Paul and Sarah. The weightlifter would no longer have to ride in buses and taxis.

Boevski decided this would be his car. The owner is happy to do a favour for the local sports star. The negotiations are short. The German offers to sell the car on credit. Galabin shakes his head. He wants to pay all at once, but asks for a couple of months to get the money.

"Kein Probleme[15]," the German replies.

***

Journalists from all over the world crowd around Boevski. He has done amazingly well. The Bulgarian has broken four world records on his way to the gold medal at the championship in Athens. Following the scenario at La Coruna, Galabin made six successful attempts in the 69 kg division. 162.5 kg on the snatch, 195 kg in the clean and jerk and a total of 357.5 kg. The last record remained unbroken for 14 years, before falling to Liao Hui of China.

"This guy is superhuman," writes a reporter of the prestigious "Associated Press" news agency. The compliments are raining down, and the interest in the Bulgarian cast a shadow over the pretender for the title in the lowest category, Halil Mutlu, who would compete for a second Olympic gold in Sydney.

"I nearly failed before the competition," Galabin admits in front of the journalists. "I used a faulty scale, which showed me two kilograms lighter. I was delighted and stuffed myself with food. It was a good thing I had enough time to lose the weight, or I would have caught fire."

The other national athletes didn't do so well in the tough competition of 395 participants. Sevdalin Minchev (62 kg) and Plamen Zhelyazkov (77 kg) win bronze medals. Ivan Ivanov (56 kg) is fourth. The rookie from

---

[15] No problem (in German)

Osetia Alan Tsagaev finishes sixth. Georgi Gardev (85 k is seventh, and Zlatan Vanev (77 kg) is ninth. Stefan Georgiev scores zero and remains out of the rankings.

***

The television station car for Northern Bulgaria "Rava TV" stops first in front of the house of Boevski family in Knezha. The table is laden with wonderful dishes, and the guests won't stop coming and going, congratulating the parents.

"We were always proud of him," smiling, Stella praises her son in front of the camera. "We are happy that his dream has come true."

The next question is for his father – Peppy. He has crossed his fingers for every competition, but refused to approve of his son's career until now.

"Galabin, I am sorry I didn't believe you, but you have proven to be a great athlete!" Peppy speaks with pride and acknowledgement in his eyes.

The camera records his revelation for all time.

***

Ivan Abadzhiev is dressed in a suit and walks precariously on the carpet of the Boyana residence. The garment seems to hang unnaturally on him. The Senior Trainer is used to wearing his favourite tracksuit. He doesn't like the camera lights and the reporters' noise and prefers looking at his notebook with the daily norms of every weightlifter.

Abadzhiata's work is gaining the respect of the journalists, who vote for him in the poll for Best Bulgarian coach of 1999. He receives the title for the third consecutive year, making a total of six in his career. The prize is a sofa suite.

The domination of weightlifting is seen in the award

for the even more prestigious title Athlete of the Year. Bulgaria's president Petar Stoyanov awards the undisputed champion for 1999 to Galabin Boevski. He is 600 points ahead, in the journalists' poll, of the World High Jump champion Hristina Kalcheva. Third is another track and field competitor – Rostislav Dimitrov. The winner receives a brand new car – a blue Peugeot 206.

***

Three days after the New Year the weightlifters are gathered together for a camp. The success in the World and European Championships in 1999 has been forgotten. Abadzhiev demands more and more brutal weights.

The cup with pills is getting fuller. Every weightlifter has a personal one. Drugs, vitamins and amino acids are taken on a schedule. The Senior Trainer and his assistants keep close watch to see that everyone is taking their medication. A war would break out if someone threw away a vitamin C pill. Abadzhiev is strict. He wants every rule he gives to be abided by. The coach is most rigorous about medication. He keeps adding more and more to the pill cups. One of them is Orocetam – a metabolic booster.

***

Georgi Gardev comes back to the room limping. A terrible pain is searing through his right knee. He sits on the bed and can barely bend it.

"I can't take it anymore," the injured weightlifter says more to himself than to Galabin, who is sitting in front of him. "I can't handle the weights with this damn knee. I will pack up my stuff. It's clear I can't do a damn thing with this injury."

"Georgi, have you gone mad? We have just a few months left until the Olympics. Hold on for just a little while," Boevski is serious.

"Galab, I will try one last thing. I need some rest. I won't make it with the maximum weights at the trials," Gardev shares his plan as he rethinks his strategy for the doctor, who everybody calls "The Help". "I will push him into giving me a pain killer in the knee and rest for a day or two."

"Abadzhiev will know you're missing straight away," the World and European champion shakes his head.

"No problem. I will take laxative and tell him I have a stomach pain. There was a virus going around recently anyway."

The trick is successful. Two days later Gardev and Galabin are taking turns on the stage. The weightlifter from Pazardzhik feels a bit better.

***

The whispering from the adjacent bed wakes up Georgi Gardev. He opens his eyes and sees Galabin, trying to say something in English. Next to him is the private tutor who used to come three times a week.

Boevski and his roommate Georgi Gardev

The drowsy weightlifter doesn't even bother to listen to the words. He turns over and tries to use the remainder of his lunch break as best he can. Gardev thinks of his friend. Besides the lessons in English, Boevski was falling asleep in the evening with a book. His speech was changing. He didn't use slang words any more. For a couple of months Galabin had been doing everything to develop intellectually.

"What's the world coming to?" Gardev thinks with a smile as he cuddles up to the soft pillow.

***

Tears are about to flow from Boevski's eyes, and his face is red. The barbell is set at 192.5 kg. A second, two and the barbell falls to the ground. The maximum weight was passed. The weightlifter is pleased. He puts some clothes on and heads for the door. The others in "Dianabad" gym continue with their attempts. Abadzhiev is writing something down in his notebook. He stops, as he sees Boevski dressed.

"Wait, where are you going?" Abadzhiev asks. "Why didn't you call me when you are going for the maximum?"

"I have already passed it, I'm not doing it again," Boevski replies, without using the required "Mister Abadzhiev" to the head coach of the national team.

"I didn't see you do it, go back," the Senior Trainer says in an icy voice.

Galabin takes in the face of the legendary mentor and heads back to the stage. On it, Georgi Gardev finishes his attempt. Boevski is mad. He puts on the weight, which he had lifted minutes ago. He has to lift, but his concentration is impaired. He fails on the first try. Abadzhiev stands next to him and pours more weight onto the barbell.

It's Gardev's turn again. The weight plates are rearranged. Two minutes later Galabin has managed to calm himself. He separates himself from everything in the gym. The attempt goes perfectly.

"There, did you see it now?" Boevski asks and leaves hastily.

His teammates can't believe it. No one has dared to oppose Abadzhiev until now.

Galabin is furious. He feels the coach doesn't like him. The weightlifter decides to act and makes a bold and decisive move. He grabs his cell phone and calls the newly elected president of the Federation, Anton Kodzhabashev. The businessman from Bourgas, who is former world champion in weightlifting, has taken the place of the representative Orlin Rizov.

"Kodzha, I can't work with Abadzhiev. Instead of lifting in peace, I'm frustrated by his presence. He keeps forcing things," sounds the angry voice of Boevski.

"Don't worry, I will look into this. You keep training as usual. I will deal with Abadzhiev," answers back the boss of Bulgarian weightlifting.

***

Georgi Gardev has no competition in his category for the European Championships in 2000, which Abadzhiev doesn't like.

"Ivan, I have one guy from Plovdiv, he is very good and is exactly in Georgi's category. Let's give him a try, so he can be his competition. I'm thinking after that to take him as a soldier into the "Levski" club," Abadzhiev's assistant Zlatin Ivanov says.

"Gardev, now you will see what this guy is going to make you look like. You won't feel very comfortable after," the Senior Trainer uses his tested trick for creating competition.

Milen Dobrev is ready for the trials. The twenty-year-old talent is preparing for his first World Championships in the seniors. He lifts an excellent, for his age, 155 and 200 kg. Gardev blows him away with 175 and 210 kg.

"Get this guy out of here. If he wants to stay, send him to sleep with the dogs," Abadzhiev is furious. The Senior Trainer points at the room, where three years ago the national team's soldier cooks were living.

Milen Dobrev refuses to sleep with the dogs. He packs his bags and takes the bus back to Plovdiv.

"Who is this guy? I give him an order, he disobeys! You won't take him in "Levski". If I see him in the army there will be terrible consequences!" shouts the head coach of the national team.

Instead of "Levski", Dobrev goes to another club - CSKA. Four years later he becomes an Olympic champion.

***

"Big Brother, you used to drive a tractor, what would you say if I offered to get you one, plus a harvester and work the land?" Galabin surprisingly asks in one of his regular talks with his uncle.

"Farming is good, but how will you find money for machines?" Hristo Boev asks.

"Don't worry. The Germans helped me a lot in choosing the machines. The municipality will rent us the land. The mayor will help, he loves weightlifting," the world champion lays out his plan.

***

The French television "Canal +" is impressed with Galabin Boevski's records. The journalists make an offer to the Bulgarian and his club trainer Plamen Asparuhov to shoot a movie in Thailand.

Abadzhiev is against the trip, because he will lose sight of his potential Olympic medalist. On the other hand, Chiang Mai is only four hours difference from Sydney and will help with getting used to the time zone. The work is going excellently, but trouble arrives unexpectedly.

"Something happened," Galabin holds his left knee after he has snatched an easy weight for him of 110kg. "It hurts like hell! I feel like my bone has been dislocated!"

The journey ends badly. At Sofia airport Hristo Boev is waiting for Galabin. He has arranged a team at Pleven's hospital. The doctors open the knee. The news is bad. A five millimeter fragment has broken off the upper part of the knee joint. The femur fracture has affected the meniscus. Galabin is desperate, but he sees hope in the eyes of Hristo Boev and Plamen Asparuhov. He is discharged after three days. One thing is certain – the European championships in Sofia will be a mirage. Only six months left until the Olympics.

***

"Naim Suleymanoglu returns," the world media explodes. The three-time Olympic champion will lift at the Sydney games. The legend will try to become the first weightlifter in history with four gold medals from the world's greatest sports forum.

The interest in Suleymanoglu is enormous. The American television stations send their teams to tell the weightlifter's amazing story. The journalists are shocked by his confession. The legend admits he was sold to Turkey for $1 250 000. The money was counted all night by representatives of the Bulgarian Federation in a hotel. There were $100 000 worth of fake bills among the genuine ones, but no one caused a problem.

The superstar's first competition after his four-year break is the European Championships in Sofia. The local reporters ask Suleymanoglu what he thinks of the scandals in the Bulgarian national team between the athletes and the coach.

"Ivan Abadzhiev is a school. It is simple – toil, discipline and persistence. That was a work model and a life style," Suleymanoglu describes the Senior Trainer simply. Under his guidance he won the last big trophy in Atlanta Olympics.

***

"Plamen, I am in great shape, I can clean and jerk 187.5 and the world record is 180," Stefan Georgiev talks on the phone. "I will defeat them all – Suleymanoglu, Peshalov and Sabanis. I just have to lose a few pounds. Let's go to sauna together."

"Come with me, we must talk," The Lizard's personal coach, "Feefee the Feather" says carefully. "I will wait for you in our café."

Georgiev senses something is happening. He has not time to wait for a bus or a taxi. He jumps straight into Georgi Gardev's car and meets Plamen Asparuhov in five minutes.

"It is proposed that you don't take part at the European championships," Asparuhov says firmly with sadness in his voice. This is a second deep disappointment for him after Boevski's injury. "Abadzhiev said so. Please, don't do anything stupid."

The Lizard doesn't say a word. The former World champion gets up and kicks the chair, which flies five meters away. He rushes back to the car and five minutes later walks into the gym. Inside Abadzhiev is making his traditional calculations after training.

"What is going on?" Stefan Georgiev turns to the head coach of the national team.

"Plamen will explain," the Senior Trainer replies without raising his head.

"Explain? Fuck you! You have done the dirty on me!" the Lizard explodes. Abadzhiev's assistants – the legendary weightlifters Andon Nikolov and Neno Terziiski grab the national athlete. The gym is full, because the teams ready to participate in the championship have arrived.

"Don't make a scene," Neno Terziiski asks, and grows red with shame.

After the European Championships, the journalist Todor Shabansky asks the Senior Trainer what the fate of Stefan Georgiev will be. The weightlifter, who is only 25 years old, has World and European titles behind him.

"As long as I am coach, he won't touch a barbell!" Abadzhiev reveals his punishment.

***

Four great weightlifters in the 62 kg division gather on the stage in Sofia. Naim Suleymanoglu, Nikolay Peshalov, Sevdalin Minchev and the veteran from Greece, Leonidas Sabanis, compete in the strongest category for many years. Three of the stars are Ivan Abadzhiev's students, but only one lifts for Bulgaria. Sevdalin Minchev finishes with a silver medal and a total of 322.5 kg. In front of him is Nikolay Peshalov, who competes for Croatia, and finishes with 325 kg. Suleymanoglu is not in good shape. He achieves a total of 310 kg, which is enough for third place. Sabanis finishes the competition without a single successful attempt.

Zlatan Vanev (77 kg) and Metin Kadir (105 kg) win gold medals. Ivan Ivanov (56 kg), Plamen Zhelyazkov (77 kg) and Georgi Gardev (85 kg) finish second in their categories.

In Boevski's division – 69kg, Abadzhiata lets in Georgi Markov for the first time. The athlete from Bourgas does excellently and gains the silver medal after six successful attempts. He ties with the champion Sergey Lavrenov, from the former Commonwealth of Independent States (CIS) – 337.5 kg. The Bulgarian is 160 grams heavier, which was decisive for the title.

***

The battle between the legends in the European Championships in Sofia puts Galabin Boevski's absence in the shadows. Many have written him off, due to his serious injury, but this motivates Knezha's hero even more. On the twentieth day he removes the braces and starts movement exercises. Then comes the mandatory check up with Dr. Rosmanov.

"You should know the knee can shut down while you lift, walk, or even go to the toilet. It will hurt a lot. It is not clear if you will recover, even if we do the surgery," the doctor speaks as he observes Boevski's reaction.

"Can I train?" Galabin asks clearly, as he felt a small hope.

"Be it on your own responsibility," the specialist replies after seeing how much Galabin believes he could prepare for the Olympics in Sydney.

***

For one week Galabin sweats under the barbell. He has returned to Knezha's gym, surprising everybody. With another lift he feels a terrible strain in the knee.

"Galabin, we have to change something," the uncle tells the weightlifter. "Your left leg is 20 centimeters thinner than the other in the thigh. You have to lift a bit heavier on one side."

"I am ready for anything, uncle Hristo. You know our dream!" Boevski replies as he rubs his broken knee.

CHAPTER VII

Half of his cellmates were coughing. Gababin's nose
was also running. The sound of the coughing continued
during the night, but the Bulgarian got used to it. He
found out from the others there was no point in calling a
doctor just for a cold. He used to come after a week,
sometimes even two for those who had flu. He had more
urgent cases – wounded prisoners with knife or glass cuts,
cracked heads after a punch up, or overdoses. Alcohol and
drugs were forbidden; at least officially. Those who had
money could get anything. Some prisoners had cellphones.
They had them secretly, because if they got caught, they
would spend a couple of days in solitary.

Galabin wondered how many times during his career
he had needed a doctor. As for injuries, he was lucky. He
had had only one, but it was very serious. It nearly ended
his career. His teammates in the national team complained
of injuries all the time. Zlatan Vanev dislocated his elbow a
couple of times. Georgi Gardev had surgery on both
knees; Milen Dobrev wrecked his lower back…

Here in prison everyone healed on their own, sooner or
later. Fevers and colds could not scare anyone. Even so,
Galabin was trying to take care of himself. He stretched

and exercised regularly. He was taking the vitamins Krasimira was bringing.

"I wonder how many similar pills I have taken," the weightlifter thought as he rolled one between his fingers.

***

The journalists had Plamen Asparuhov surrounded. The coach of the strongest club in Bulgaria "Ladimex" (Pernik) was being attacked by clever questions. The star in the juniors Damian Damianov was put in prison, after being sentenced on charges of assault and battery of a businessman. The medalist from the last two Olympics, Yoto Yotov, was lured by Nikolay Peshalov to lift for Croatia. Stefan Georgiev was thrown out of the national team for swearing at Ivan Abadzhiev and Bulgaria's top athlete, Galabin Boevski, was recovering from a serious injury.

"There is a lot of time until the games in Sydney," Plamen Asparuhov defends himself. "Our club's president – Lucy Stoykov - will donate a brand new modern Mercedes if one of our boys becomes an Olympic champion!"

The next day the burly businessman, whose revenue increased by millions of Deutschmarks every month, calls Feefee the Feather.

"Plamen, what are these things in the newspapers? I just found out I am donating a Mercedes," Lucy Stoykov laughs. For him such an expense is a flea bite. "Our boys are all scattered around. Who is going to win the Olympic title?"

***

Boevski had already arrived in Sofia. He managed to change his lifting technique, with the help of his uncle. The results increase steadily. Under the guidance of Plamen

Asparuhov, Galabin improves even further. However, they are still far behind his results from last year. Ivan Abadzhiev notices that every week the weightlifter is getting closer to his colleagues. The decision has been made. Boevski is going to the last camp with the team, before the final acclimatisation training in Malaysia.

"Mister Abadzhiev, why are we going all the way to Montana," Zlatan Vanev asks. He is considered one of the contenders for a gold medal, after winning two of the last three World Championships and triumphing with a European title last month.

"We will hide from the doping police," the Senior Trainer answers jokingly, but also seriously.

Actually his goal is different all together.

***

The national athletes are staying in a chalet, located in the border zone. The doping police show up on the first day. The scared weightlifters look at Abadzhiev, but his face is absolutely clear of worry.

"Okay, mister Abadzhiev, why did you bring us to this godforsaken village?" Zlatan Vanev wonders. "Today the locals showed us where the bombs fell, from the war in Serbia. There is no place for us to even drink a coffee."

"That is exactly why we came here," The Senior Trainer starts to explain. "Imagine you go to a café. You order, and someone suffering from hepatitis has been drinking there. They hadn't washed up the cup, and what happens? You get back to the camp and infect everybody and that's it – no way for us to go to the Olympics."

***

The biggest winner of Abadzhiev's secluded camp is the chalet manager. The astute caretaker has put in a blue fixed "Betacom" phone. Everyone was calling friends, coaches, families, because there was nothing for them to do in their spare time.

"This guy must have made 10 000 levs from phone cards," Georgi Gardev thinks as he heard the phone ring. Someone had dialed the number from outside.

"Mister Abadzhiev, it's for you," the chalet manager takes the call, as he finishes his fourth rakia. The voice of the seasoned drinker is surprisingly serious. "I think it's the president."

The Senior Trainer jumps up. He heads towards the phone with his back as straight like a soldier.

"Yes mister president, no mister president. We have everything," Abadzhiev answers before the eyes of the astonished national athletes.

The president of Bulgaria, Petar Stoyanov, had decided to check on the country's golden team, as everyone expected eight medals from eight weightlifters in the Olympics.

***

Boevski throws the towel to the other end of the bed and lies on the pillow. He just got out of the bathroom. The good news is the training for today is over. The bad news is that at the other end of the room Georgi Gardev is snoring louder than a tractor in Knezha.

Galabin reaches out with his right arm and grabs the magazine lying on his sport bag. A brand new grey Mercedes C-Class shines on the cover. The weightlifter had not forgotten Lucy Stoykov's promise. He had sold the Peugeot, received as an award for Athlete of the Year and drove around in his favourite VW Golf. He already knew enough German to read the magazine. Inside it said you had to wait six months after placing an order for the luxurious car.

"No problem, as long as it's automatic," the weightlifter dreamed.

***

The camp in Malaysia was the last stage of the national team's training for the Olympics in Sydney. The Bulgarian stars are lifting record weights every day. The stress is not so intense anymore. However, Ivan Abadzhiev wants their good results to become stable. He decides it is not good enough and sees the weightlifters one by one in his room.

"Georgi, what's going on?" Boevski can't wait to question his friend, who returns from his meeting with Abadzhiata.

"He offered me some stuff, ampoules, but I don't know what it was. I refused. Now he is asking for you, Galab," Gardev replies.

The weightlifter from Knezha heads for Abadzhiev's room. Their relationship is not good. The coach accepted he could not control Boevski's training.

Norayr Nurikyan (in the middle) is trying to make peace between Ivan Abadzhiev and Galabin Boevski

The specialist knows it's better to leave alone one of his potential medalists, as long as he lifts well in training.

There is one more man in the Senior Trainer's office – the general secretary of the Federation, Norair Nurikyan.

"Are you going to use this stuff?" Abadzhiev asks and points at a box.

The name of the drug is obscured by medical tape. There is one ampoule outside the pack, also unidentified.

"No, because I don't know what it is. I don't want anything from you. I take whatever I need," Boevski replies directly.

"Wait, wait, coach, prepare one for him," Nurikyan tries to defuse the tension.

"If he doesn't want it, I won't force him," the legendary coach mutters feeling insulted.

A couple of minutes later, Boevski returns to the gym. Gardev raises a questioning eyebrow.

"Fuck him! I refused too," Galabin laughs.

***

"Today I am disappointed by Gardev and Galabin's behaviour," Ivan Abadzhiev begins the evening talk.

The two weightlifters are over it. They are already in Malaysia and there is no way for The Senior Trainer to get back at them. If they were in Bulgaria, they may have thought of taking the medication. The risk was that they would be thrown out of the team straight away, despite their results during training. The stand of The Lizard came to mind. Stefan Georgiev got expelled for swearing, and he was almost certain to compete in Sydney.

"These athletes refused to take the medication I offered," The Senior Trainer goes on. "Because they are very smart and know everything, very soon they will discover they are not so smart after all, when they go to the Olympics and fail."

For Abadzhiev a bad performance was to finish fourth, and sometimes not to finish first.

"From now on, I take no responsibility for them," the coach continues his scolding. "They may do whatever they want. They will be responsible for the failure!"

"Well fine, there is nothing more to say," Gardev replies, after exchanging a glance with his friend. "It's all clear. We don't think it is necessary for us to attend the meeting, if you don't find us interesting and don't wish to make any more comments to us."

***

The cunning fox Norair Nurikyan hasn't given up. He is a lot more diplomatic than the despotic Ivan Abadzhiev. With pleas and jokes he managed to persuade the two rebels.

"Boys, this is a powerful weapon. It's called Orocetam, and will give you a lot of power," Nurikyan starts, but fails again. "Come on, how long do I have to argue with you? Tomorrow I want you to try it."

"Norair, I start to feel uncomfortable with you on our backs all the time," Gardev says, laughing. "Honestly, tomorrow I am going to try it. I will prove to you it doesn't work. I have already taken this in Bulgaria. Abadzhiev stuck 3-4 shots of that stuff up my backside, and the usual dosage is one. Then I felt my brain moving. I felt as if I had hit my head against the wall, I'll get a hole in my forehead. On top of all after that I got injured and my knee started to hurt."

Galabin also agrees only to satisfy Nurikyan.

***

"Coach, go on, prepare two doses," says Nurikyan, who brought in Galabin and Gardev.

"Well they are not here yet," Abadzhiev replies, seeing

the two weightlifters at the door.

"Prepare two shots I tell you," Nurikyan raises his hand.

"Prepare for whom?" The coach continues to play dumb.

"For these two," the Federation's general secretary is persistent.

"Well they don't want it," the Senior Trainer continues to play his role of the aggrieved party.

"Now, if I tell you something, you do it," Nurikyan finishes, as he comes closer to the table.

Abadzhiev smiles, pulls out the box with Orocetam and fills two shots. He has won the psychological battle.

***

Before training Galabin and Gardev sit down for a cola and coffee, to wake themselves up. This would be their first exercise since Abadzhiev's improvised laboratory.

"Damn it Galab, I feel very strange," Gardev shakes his head. "Did we mess something up? It can't be the coffee, we drink it every day."

"Let's go straight to the gym," Boevski offers.

As always, the two of them are on the same stage. After the warm up, Gardev lifted 150 kg as an initial weight, as he usually snatches without trouble. Several months earlier in the European Championships in Sofia he achieved 175 kg. Galabin's friend gets under the barbell. It's moving back and forth. His elbow shakes. The weightlifter drops the barbell.

"Galab, I don't know what I am doing and where I am," Gardev holds his head. Galabin, who is also in the lighter division, grabs the barbell after him. He lifts 130 kg, which is 30 kilograms lighter than his best result. The effect is the same. An unsuccessful attempt and a shaking of hands.

"I'm going to try 160 kg," Gardev decides to go for an

increase. "Perhaps the weight is too light for me and I underestimated it."

The lift begins. Gardev grabs the barbell, stands still and starts to think; something unnatural for weightlifters. For them an attempt on heavy weights should be automatic, trained to the very last bend of the joints. Otherwise failure is certain. And this is what happens. Gardev raises the barbell to his pelvis and drops it.

"I won't lift in this event anymore, I am going to injure myself," Georgi shakes his head. Galabin doesn't give up so easy. He tries the second event – clean and jerk. He puts 170 kg, because he sees that on the neighbouring stage his competitor in the same category, Georgi Markov lifts like a beast. His impotence is doubled after Galabin barely turns the barbell in the first part of the attempt. He finishes it with a great effort.

"Sod this, we are going to wreck ourselves," Georgi Gardev wipes away the sweat, as he thinks how much work he has wasted for an injection. A little earlier he tried the second event, the clean and jerk with the measly weight of 90 kg. Then he feels the medication's effect even stronger. His arms bend, and he feels as if the barbell with go through him, cutting him in half.

"That's it boys, you won't take any more of it," Norair Nurikyan fumes walking around the two weightlifters. "It's all my fault."

***

At the evening meeting sparks fly between Abadzhiev and the two rebels.

"You are simulating," the national team's head coach spits fire. "Do you know how good this stuff is? The professor who invented it is like an animal in the bedroom, despite his old age. He experimented with mice, which have an incredible capacity for work. If you take it, no one would be able to come within 5-10 kg of you."

Boevski and Gardev don't know where they are. They decide to skip one day of training to recover from the effects of the medication, which is taken daily by the rest of the squad. The missed day is extremely important for the training, because it breaks the set regime of the last months.

***

The pain in Boevski's knee grows. He tries to reduce the load, but he knows it would be fatal for his performance on the Olympics.

"Plamen, my knee is blocked," Galabin gives his regular report to his coach in "Ladimex". It must have been the climate change. I'm thinking of quitting the Olympics.

"Look, the easiest thing is to quit," Asparuhov reacts. "Try everything possible, because you may be sorry."

"Okay, I will try, and let us play it by ear."

A couple of hours later the same words are heard on the phone between Kuala Lumpur and Knezha.

"Big Brother, I am leaving." The World and European champion is convinced by the increasing pain.

"Are you insane? At least go and watch it. You have come this far, and now you want to come back?" Hristo Boev insists.

The words of his coaches make Galabin steel himself.

***

A couple of days after the injection Galabin and Gardev are back on the stage together. Zlatan Vanev and Georgi Markov are taking turns next to them. They are making successful attempts one after another. It's Vanev's turn. He has lifted 167.5 kg for the snatch. This is the maximum weight he has managed to lift to date. The European champion gets under the barbell and at this exact moment his elbow clicks. The barbell falls back. If Shakespeare had seen Vanev's look in this exact moment, he would have rewritten "Romeo and Juliet". The Olympics for him are over and his elbow joint is dislocated for the second time.

Another hope for a medal – Plamen Zhelyazkov tears a muscle. Sevdalin Minchev gets knee pains. The weightlifters clench their teeth in the name of the Olympic Hope, despite the danger of crippling themselves.

***

"That's enough, now you just have to be careful," says the former World champion Neno Terziiski turning towards Gardev. The mentor is responsible for Georgi, Galabin Boevski, Ivan Ivanov and Sevdalin Minchev. The weightlifter had just made a total of 400 kg. The achievement is 10 kg above the world record in the 85 kg division. The talent from Pazardzhik is pleased. The medal is assured, and the title looks real. On the way out of the gym he passes Ivan Abadzhiev.

"Gardev, join me for a moment, I want to talk to you about something," The Senior Trainer says, as the weightlifter pulls up a chair. "Why do you react so sharply to my suggestions? Look how strong you are, and your results. Don't reject the medication. You don't know what will happen to you at the Olympics. Start taking it again, I will give you two ampoules, four may be too much for you."

"Okay, you saw, just now, I got an excellent result, which could make me an Olympic champion, and you are trying to speak to me again," Georgi Gardev begins. He let Abadzhiev go on speaking, because he was still out of breath from the big attempt. "You want to be close to me, so tomorrow, when I come first you can say you were next to me, and if I fail, you can tell me how smart I am. Why are you promoting this medication, as if I am going to wrestle bears? You were eloquent enough at the meetings, for me to understand you don't care about my progress. There is nothing more for us to say to one another. Since I am responsible for myself, I think I don't need that. If I am wrong, it would be my fault."

The Senior Trainer only looked at Gardev and remained silent. He had decided to try the same tactic with Boevski too, but understood that if he tried, he could be sworn at.

"Damn me, you put him in his place," Galabin laughs loudly, as they get back to their room.

"I don't hate Abadzhiev, I just don't feel comfortable with these injections," Gardev says. "Twice we had high risk situations, and we almost injured ourselves."

***

At the first entry into the Olympic village, the national athletes are lined up to give samples. The Bulgarians arrive late at night, and find the doping cops waiting in the morning. All tests are negative. This is the second one for this month. The weightlifters are calm and ready to destroy their competition in the largest sports forum in Sydney.

On the first day – Monday, Ivan Abadzhiev is very happy. Izabela Rifatova is first in the women's category of 48 kg. Ivan Ivanov (56 kg) is second after the incredible Halil Mutlu. Everything is going perfectly.

On Tuesday it will be Sevdalin Minchev's turn in the 62 kg division. Immediately prior to his participation they receive bad news. Rifatova and Ivanov's samples are positive for the diuretic Furosemide in the doping test. They are disqualified and their medals immediately taken away. Despite the tension, Minchev finishes third in his category. Another Bulgarian is champion – Nikolay Peshalov, who competes for Croatia. The legend Naim Suleymanoglu fails. He scores zero, and leaves the stage forever.

***

The result of Minchev's positive doping test comes out one hour before the battle in the 69 kg division, which would be on Wednesday. He is found with Furosemide as well, Galabin Boevski and Georgi Markov hear the news as they were still at the weigh in.

The rules of the International Weightlifting Federation (IWF) state, that if there are three athletes caught from one team, then all members are stopped from competing. The decision must be taken by the officials of the IWF. The chiefs don't have enough time to discuss it before Boevski's and Markov's participation. Luckily for the Bulgarians the meeting is scheduled for the next day – Thursday, which is a rest day in weightlifting.

***

Georgi Markov starts the competition very strongly. The 22-year-old weightlifter sets a world record of 165 kg in the first event – the snatch. Galabin makes three successful attempts, but his best is 162.5 kg. He is dressed in a red leotard with dark stripes down the middle, different from the outfits of the other national athletes.

Ivan Abadzhiev is not in the hall. He has isolated himself in the Olympic village after the shameful disqualification of the three athletes. Instead of him, the weightlifters are brought to the stage by the president of the Bulgarian Weightlifting Federation, Anton Kodzhabashev.

Boevski is not worried by the setback in the first event. He starts strongly in the clean and jerk with 185 kg. Markov lifts the barbell first at 182.5 and then at 187.5 kg. His third attempt of 192.5 kg is unsuccessful. Even if he had been successful, he would not have been able to get the gold. Boevski makes an amazing lift of 190 kg. He already knows he is an Olympic champion, because he is lighter than his competitor. Despite that, he announces he will go for a staggering 196.5 kg. Galabin raises the barbell onto his chest. He jerks it up, and leans the weight to his right leg to protect the operated knee. The barbell is above his head, and his strong arms lock it in place.

With a total of 359 kg the boy, who 14 years earlier wanted to be like Maradona, is now an Olympic champion, and with two world records – in the clean and jerk and the total. The happy winner gets up and kisses his knee.

**

On Thursday morning the meeting of the International Federation begins. It is decided Ivan Abadzhiev's team will be prevented from competing. The manager of the Bulgarian Olympic Committee Ivan "Bateto" Slavkov, who five years later was removed from the Olympic movement due to corruption charges, acts very energetically. He orders all medication to be tested, in order to locate the source of the Furosemide. He files a request to the Court of Arbitration for Sports to get the team back into the Games. There are three Bulgarian competitors left to participate by the end of the weightlifting competitions. Plamen Zhelyazkov (77 kg) is supposed to get on the stage on Friday, on Saturday Georgi Gardev (85 kg) and on Monday – Alan Tsagaev (105 kg).

**

The tests show, that the amount of the forbidden substance in the bodies of the Bulgarians who have been caught is minimal – 0.03 micrograms per milliliter above the norm. A month later the specialists in Bulgaria calculate, that if Ivan Ivanov, Izabela Rifatova and Sevdalin Minchev had urinated between the events, the

After the winning lift in Sydney

tests would have been negative. Unfortunately by that time the three were drained by rigorous weight loss in the last days before the Olympics. The water enters the body, but the organism doesn't discard it right away, because it is uncertain if it will receive fluids in the next couple of days.

***

Georgi Markov passes. His sample and Galabin's are clear. The man from Bourgas followed Abadzhiev's advice 100% and took the same medication as Ivan Ivanov, Sevdalin Minchev and Izabela Rifatova. But Markov is afraid of needles. That's why he took the Orocetam orally. Abadzhiev's ambition to defeat Galabin Boevski, who uses his own methods to train, makes The Senior Trainer send Markov into the lower category. For this he loses 7-8 kilograms in the last weeks before the Olympics.

Absolutely dehydrated a day before the competition, the weightlifter decides not to drink the nasty powder, because after that he would have to rinse his mouth with juice. The sweet liquid will increase the need for water, which may jeopardize falling within the category. The decision has been made – he would not drink Orocetam. On the day of the event, the national team's doctor forgets about the medication. Markov skips his dose again.

***

The fallout from the scandal with the positive tests is the leading news in Sydney. The Bulgarian athletes, recognizable by their outfits, are branded as criminals by their colleagues.

On Thursday the bus from the Olympic village to the training gym is full. Georgi Gardev senses he is being pointed at, and a centre of attention. However, he doesn't lose hope.

On the training stage Georgi meets his main rival in his

division, Pyrros Dimas. He is getting ready to attack the Olympic title, and the Bulgarian is his most serious opponent. The weightlifter from Pazardzhik tries to isolate himself from the tension, but out of the corner of his eye he sees Dimas's phone ring. The Greek answers, exchanges a few words and looks at him smiling.

"Georgi, you have been shut down," quietly whispers the Qatar team's coach Zlatin Ivanov, who had approached unnoticed. Gardev understands his rival's happiness.

Boevski speaking on the phone. Plamen Zhelyazkov with hat, right of him sitting down is Nikolay Peshalov, who won gold for Croatia. The last on the right is Georgi Markov, who still holds the world record in the snatch in the 69 kg division.

***

Abadzhiev's assistants Andon Nikolov and Neno Terziiski go to get Plamen Zhelyazkov and head for the competition hall. It's time for his category. No one has announced officially if the Bulgarian weightlifters can participate, because everyone is awaiting Bateto's plea to the arbitration jury to give some result any moment. Georgi Gardev can't enjoy Galabin's title, because he continually wonders if he is going to participate or not. He decides to distract from the tension. He lifts some weighs in the gym and goes back. He showers, shaves and plans to take a walk to his favourite barbeque in the Olympic village, where they make unique beef steaks.

On his way out he meets Plamen Zhelyazkov, who has his hat on backwards. He viciously kicks the door, and his bag gets caught in the frame.

"What is going on?" Gardev asks carefully.

"What do you think? I defeated them, and now I'm going back," Zhelyazkov answers sharply.

"When did you defeat them?" Georgi tries to get some information, because he knows his colleague's competition starts in an hour.

"And where are you going?" Furious, Zhelyazkov returns a question, without giving an answer.

"I'm going to the scale and then to get something to eat," Gardev senses what is going on.

"You can just go back," his colleague mercilessly sticks a knife in his bubble of hope. "The competition is over for me and for you. When I went to the weigh in, I got kicked out. They didn't even let me watch. They threw me out of the hall."

***

On Saturday Gardev watches on the small screen as Pyrros Dimas becomes Olympic champion for the third time. He wins with a total of 390 kg. Two weeks earlier the Bulgarian scored 400 kg in training.

It wasn't until Monday, when Bateto wins the case in the Court of Arbitration for Sports and returns the team's competing privileges. Alan Tsagaev (105 kg) gets his chance. His last attempt in the clean and jerk is for the Olympic title. Because of all the stress around, the pulling out and return of the weightlifters, his nerves fail. He fouls at 237.5 kg, but with the results so far wins a silver medal.

"Galab, look how the fate is such an interesting thing," Georgi Gardev laughs with regret.

The Olympic champion has nothing to say. He prefers to keep silent.

***

At Sofia's airport the mood is ranging from one extreme to the other. The journalists have circled Ivan Abadzhiev. He looks distraught, as if he would start crying at any moment. He blames the supply company of Orocetam – "Sofarma" for not listing Furosemide in the table of contents. It is unclear how it got into the medication. The Bulgarian Olympic Committee, the Weightlifting Federation, athletes and coaches file a lawsuit against the pharmaceutical giant. The investigation concludes there are no traces of Furosemide in the Orocetam taken from the drug stores after the scandal. The official version for the contamination is an uncleaned ampoule packaging machine. Nine years after the Olympics in Sydney, "Sofarma" wins the lawsuit in the high court, disappointing Abadzhiev and the weightlifters.

"When the journalists see this guy, they will probably think what kind of freaks the weightlifters are for draining the life out of him and it is exactly the other way around," the most disadvantaged man in the whole affair, Georgi Gardev, turns his eyes for the last time towards The Senior Trainer, and heads with broken dreams to the taxi, parked in front of Sofia airport.

***

Boevski's face can't be seen amongst the heap of bouquets. His friends have multiplied every day since he started winning medals in major competitions. The number of people who were with him 4-5 years ago could be counted on the fingers of one hand. Then his pockets were empty, and he was travelling free on public transport.

The weightlifter is hugging little Sarah. Her Big Brother Paul is spinning like a top from happiness. Krasimira sheds a tear and leaves her partner to the reporters. She knows she will enjoy being with him later.

Plamen Asparuhov is also thrilled. His athlete is one of the five Bulgarian Olympic champions in Sydney. The trainer from Pernik becomes a favourite to succeed Ivan Abadzhiev, as the coach hinted he would resign, because of the doping scandal.

Hristo Boev waits in one of the corners of the airport. When the crowd of reporters and welcoming people around the gold medalist disperse, the champion heads in that direction.

"We did it, Big Brother," Galabin says as he hugs his uncle. Their common dream has become became a reality.

CHAPTER VIII

Galabin turned the next page, sitting comfortably outside, far from the nasty cell, in which even the light was poisonous. About ten languages could be heard in the jail yard. Almost everyone knew Portuguese. Boevski understood most of the words. Even so, he preferred to read Bulgarian. Since he arrived in Itai, he wanted only one thing from his relatives – to send him books in his native language. Krasimira brought packages with different titles. Most of all he liked biographies of athletes, artists, and all kinds of successful people.

He knew the book selection was made by the fitness manager, Tsvetelina. One day he decided to donate all his books in Bulgarian to the library. There were several Bulgarians in the prison. He didn't avoid them, but also had no intention of creating new friendships in this place filled with criminals.

He had been all over the world and was able to read people like a book. During the World Championships in Turkey, they wanted to rip him apart, when he defeated their favourite. A lot of people would break up at a moment like that, but he didn't. He felt something similar behind bars. The weak ones had the smell of fear. The predators could feel it and took advantage by racketeering for cigarettes, other items or brutal physical assaults. They kept away from him. They could see subdued rage in his eyes. A wolf, locked in a cage.

***

Bulgaria's president, Petar Stoyanov is disappointed. The politician with the constant grin has forgotten his smile. He is the host of the "Athlete of the Year" awards, but blushes with shame, when three of the Olympic champions miss the ceremony. Tanyu Kiryakov, who won a second gold medal from the world's largest sports forum, had a high fever and was unable to unlock his vehicle. His colleague from the shooting sport Maria Grozdeva had car trouble on her way back from the sea. Galabin's excuse is that one of his children is ill.

All journalists are aware of the boycott. In the poll, first place goes to Tereza Marinova, the triple jump star. Second is Tanyu Kiryakov and third is the weightlifter. After him are the other two Bulgarian Olympic champions – the wrestler Armen Nazaryan and Maria Grozdeva.

***

Plamen Asparuhov is appointed as coach of the national weightlifting team. Abadzhiev leaves for Qatar, where he prepares the local weightlifters. Feefee the Feather finds the ruins of a team. Zlatan Vanev and Metin Kadir had not yet recovered from their injuries. The Olympic Games silver medalist Alan Tsagaev is in terrible shape. Galabin Boevski decided to take a rest from two years of constant camps and competitions.

Only eight weightlifters show up in the gym, which narrows the selection appreciably. The lack of competition is a reason for the results in the European Championships in Trencin (Slovakia) – only two silver medals. The awards go to Georgi Gardev, who lifts with a cracked wrist, and Nikolay Stoyanov. Stefan Georgiev – The Lizard - returns to the team with a fourth place.

***

With a 60 000 levs state bonus for the gold from the Olympics and 10 000 levs from the Weightlifting Federation, the money won by Galabin was not enough for him even to buy an apartment[16]. The Mercedes from Lucy Stoykov arrived from Germany a couple of months ago. The weightlifter was already thinking about selling it. He does so a year later.

Boevski lives in a rented flat near the "Vitosha" shoe factory. Armen Nazaryan, the wrestler is his neighbour. Stella Boevski moves from Knezha to Sofia, so she can help Krasimira with her wild kids, when it was time for the weightlifter to start going to camps.

***

"Chief, I am sending Galabin to train with you," the deep voice of Yani "Marchoka" Marchokov, one of the weightlifters sold to Qatar, comes through on the telephone. "He has a quarrel with Feefee the Feather and Kodzhabashev."

"How can he come to me, if he has trainers?" the coach of Sofia's "Slavia" club, Ludmil Kochev, replies. The specialist trained Marchoka for many years.

"It's ok, he makes his own plans for training. You just have to keep him company in the gym so he is not alone."

"How are things with you? How's Qatar?" Kochev asks.

"How do you think? I had a quarrel with Abadzhiev.

---

[16] During this time 3 levs were equal to 2 dollars

We had a fist fight," replies Boevski's classmate from "Olympic Hopes. "I am coming back to train with you."

***

Ludmil Kochev's house is 500 meters away from Galabin Boevski's apartment. Every day the weightlifter goes to the coach of "Slavia" and from there the two of them head to the gym.

"Why don't you want to be in the national team?" Kochev asks surprisingly.

"I am tired of those pointless camps," Galabin replies. "I want to be closer to my family. My children are growing up and I am always away. The training sessions get too stretched in the national team. I want to work intensively, to do my thing and go. No jokes, messing around and discussions."

"You are right. Are you going to light one, before we go?" Kochev asks, knowing the weightlifter's bad habit.

"No, I stopped after the Olympics," Boevski shakes his head. "I promised myself if I won the title I would never light up again. When we left for Australia I had a couple of cigarette packs. I gave the remaining ones to the other Bulgarians after I won the gold."

***

The Sabanci family are among the richest people in Turkey. A member of the millionaire clan built a sports hall in the Antalya resort. It is in honour of his daughter, who is confined to a wheelchair. The first big event to take place in it is the World Weightlifting Championships. After the feeble performance in the European Championships, Plamen Asparouhov has his back to the wall.

"I'm not yet ready to compete," Galabin Boevski, who had started training a couple of months ago, admits.

"You have to help me. I need you, or they will kick me

The rich businessman Lucy Stoykov rewarded Boevski with a brand new Mercedes for the Olympic gold

out. It is very difficult to assemble a team, since Abadzhiev sold half of our national athletes to Qatar," Plamen Asparuhov uses his most plaintive voice.

"Alright, I'll lift, but don't expect anything great from me." Boevski had not forgotten the hard years, when Feefee the Feather helped by taking him into his club "Ladimex".

***

Three thousand five hundred Turks are yelling as if they had just heard the news of the Veliko Tarnovo siege during the time of the second Bulgarian kingdom[17]. There are only 2500 seats in the hall. The rest of the spectators are standing. Fights are breaking out here and there, because someone stepped on his neighbour. The police are powerless.

Reyhan Arabacioglu makes a wonderful performance in the snatch in the 69 kg category. He lifts 155 kg – five more than the Olympic champion Galabin Boevski and the veteran Giorgios Tzelilis. The Bulgarian doesn't look worried, even though he has had only one successful attempt until then. He knows his most powerful event is coming up – the clean and jerk. In contrast, Plamen Asparuhov is sweating, nervously wringing his hands. He lit a cigarette in the hall and was fined 100 dollars.

"180 kg" lights up on the board. Arabacioglu, Boevski and Tzelilis lift it. The Turk ends at this weight, but the Greek lifts 185 kg. In his second attempt, Galabin cleans and jerks 187.5 kg whilst the spectators boo loudly. According to an unwritten rule in weightlifting, the audience must be completely silent during the lifts. In Turkey these regulations don't apply, and even the guards

---

[17] A key moment in Bulgarian history, after which Bulgaria lost its independence to Turkey for five centuries.

can't shut 3500 throats up. Tzelilis fails at this weight, which means the Bulgarian is champion. The fanatics had still not settled down after their hero failed.

"Plamen, tell them to put on 190 kg," Boevski says in a firm, wolf-like voice to the happy coach, who can't believe the competition's incredible twist.

"Wait, there is no point," Asparuhov is surprised. "You have already won the title, and the record is 196.5 kg. Don't tease them. It can get dangerous."

"Put it on, I tell you!" Boevski is firm and heads towards the stage.

"Gyaur, gyaur[18]," the frantic crowd swear and boo the Bulgarian. With the barbell in his hands, Galabin has distanced himself from his surroundings. For him, the only thing that matters is the lift. He raises the barbell on his chest, lifts it a couple of centimeters above his head and holds it.

A second later Boevski sticks his chest out and makes the sign Hulk Hogan used when he became a legend in wrestling. His hand becomes an extension of his ear, and its meaning is clear – "I can't hear you".

At this moment, it was as if 3500 Turkish tongues had been cut off.

***

The Lizard and Milen Dobrev are the other two medalists from the World Championships. They win bronze medals. Plamen Zhelyazkov and Nikolay Stoyanov finish fourth, and the others are far from their best shape.

Under Ivan Abadzhiev's management, the Qataris, who are competing with only three athletes, win two world

---

[18] Gyaur – a synonym for a slave, used for the Christian population in the Ottoman Empire, and also for those from European countries and Russia.

titles, thanks to Andrey Ivanov and Yani Marchokov. The Arabic country is first in the medals ratings. Both champions are richly rewarded. The Senior Trainer proves once again that his controversial methods of training get results. The impact is even stronger on Plamen Asparuhov, because not long ago Andrey Ivanov was training under him, without achieving anything this big.

After the competition Marchoka admits he is in conflict with Abadzhiev. He refuses to train under him.

In Bulgaria, Anton Kodzhabashev leaves Plamen Asparuhov as head of the national team mostly because of Galabin's title.

***

Galabin stops the Mercedes in front of Ludmil Kochev's house. He reaches into the boot and gets the carp out. The fishing trip was successful. Sarah and Paul jump out of the back seats and head in search of hidden treasures in the yard.

"I convinced Plamen there is no need for me to go to camps. He knows I can prepare myself successfully," Boevski says to Kochev, who is more a friend to him, than a coach.

"That's good," the trainer of "Slavia" confirms. "As long as you feel okay with individual training, things will happen."

The subject changes quickly. They talk of everyday things, politics, and the rise of the general secretary of the Ministry of Internal Affairs, Boiko Borisov, who has just been promoted from colonel to major general. Meanwhile Krasimira and Kochev's wife are working on the carp, and the kids manage to get dirty.

***

Six months after the world title, Boevski and the national team return to Antalya. It is time for the European Championship. This time Plamen Asparuhov has assembled a very strong team. Galabin wins the title very convincingly. He lifts 17.5 kg in the total score more than the second athlete – Tzelilis. His recent competitor Georgi Markov has been moved to the upper category – 77 kg, where he becomes champion. Zlatan Vanev finishes second. The third title is won by Alan Tsagaev (105 kg). Stefan Georgiev (62 kg) and Milen Dobrev (94 kg) return home with silver medals. At the beginning of 2002, Bulgaria is again the leading European power in weightlifting.

***

The community centre in Knezha is bursting. More people push to get in from outside. Galabin Boevski holds a speech. Short and clear. He expresses his gratitude to his parents and coaches. His uncle, Hristo Boev is proud. In the last three years the man from Knezha is undefeated in competitions he has participated in. He had become the most popular man in the region.

"Big Brother Hristo, I want to start a business," Galabin tells him, when the two of them head back home. "With the money from farming I want to build a nice, modern bar in the town, because there never was one here. Will you help me? I will be training in Sofia."

"You can count on me," Hristo Boev accepts.

***

Galabin's popularity rises with every victory. The television networks' sportscasts compete to invite him as guest. He feels the time for him to leave the gym approaches.

"Please, at least come during the last weeks to train with us," Plamen Asparuhov says, sensing the first signs of star sickness. "I will leave you to train as you wish. We shall transfer the money for training directly to you."

"Don't worry. There is no one else besides me who can get a medal in the World Championship in Warsaw," the Olympic champion replies.

***

At the height of summer, the apartment of the Boevski family is robbed. Most of the awards are stolen – the gold medal from the Olympics in Sydney and the trophies from the World and European Championships.

"It hurts me deeply, but there are worse ills than these. I don't want the people to feel sorry for me, and say "Poor guy, what a terrible tragedy has befallen him"," Boevski admits in an interview for the "Sega" newspaper two months later.

The weightlifter decides to replace the rich medals collection with another one. He starts collecting elephant figurines in different materials from the countries he visits.

***

"Big Brother Hristo, I have a temperature of 42 degrees, I don't know if I should go on the stage in Warsaw at all," Galabin Boevski admits on the telephone to his coach Hristo Boev.

"You must not give up. You know what everybody would think if you quit at the last moment, right?" Hristo Boev reasons on the telephone. "There is still time, the doctor will bring the fever down."

Ludmil Kochev drives the weightlifter to the airport in his car. He feels, that in the last few days of training, things are not going in their traditionally smooth manner. The failed attempts are too many, which frustrates the weightlifter. The experienced coach of "Slavia" is worried, but doesn't dare say out loud that Galabin is not in shape.

***

The battle for the title begins very poorly for Boevski. He makes only one successful attempt in the snatch – 150 kg. For the first time since he has been participating in major senior championships, the talented man from Knezha is looking unfocused. Plamen Asparuhov is worried.

Things are even worse in the clean and jerk. Galabin starts riskily with a very heavy weight - 187.5 kg. He will risk it, because he is after the title or nothing at all. Three unsuccessful attempts and zero. Boevski's winning streak is finished.

Galabin and his collection of elephant figurines

Contrary to his forecasts, the other national weightlifters are having amazing performances. Georgi Markov (77 kg) and Zlatan Vanev (85 kg) are world champions. Milen Dobrev (94 kg), Alan Tsagaev (105 kg) and, returning after prison, Damian Damianov (105 kg) win silver. Stefan "The Lizard" Georgiev (62 kg) is third. Boevski and the other one dropping out with zero, Plamen Zhelyazkov, are the only ones failing to win a medal.

***

"Boevski quits weightlifting", "Bulgaria's golden boy finishes his career", "Galabin says it's over," these are just some of the headlines in the Bulgarian press after the competition. The night after the failure, the weightlifter stands before the journalists and admits he cried for 20 minutes in the dressing room.

"After this failure I am cutting short my career for one year. Actually, I am considering ending it forever," Galabin throws in the bomb. "I don't want to see a barbell for at least three months. I was not prepared. I was pushed to participate. Training was going well, I was in shape, but suddenly my results started dropping down. I wonder if I would ever be able to recover from this crash. Now I don't have the strength and ambition to start again."

***

The year before the 2004 Olympics is very important. The World Championships in Vancouver are a decisive qualification for the games in Athens. The season starts well for Boevski. Just five months after the Championships in Warsaw he returns to train with Plamen Asparuhov. The two of them had a down to earth conversation after the failure, which changed the weightlifter's attitude towards training.

The mood is excellent in the "Dianabad" gym. All the

big stars and champions had gathered. Boevski has one aim. He wants to break Georgi Markov's record in the snatch from the Olympics – 165 kg. It is the only record in the category that does not belong to Galabin.

"What happened?" Plamen Asparuhov jumps up from the chair a moment after Boevski dropped the barbell, holding his elbow. The head coach of the national team throws a quick look at the barbell on the stage and counts the weights – 170 kg.

"I think I am injured, I have to see a doctor," Galabin, who had lifted the weight a couple of days earlier, replies.

The trauma isn't very serious, but it is enough to stop the star's ambition of breaking the record at the upcoming European championships.

***

The Greek town of Loutraki is another place where the Bulgarian anthem is frequently heard. Galabin Boevski is in excellent shape and has no competition for the title. Georgi Markov, Zlatan Vanev, and Milen Dobrev are the other three gold medalists. Stefan Georgiev and Alan Tsagaev are second. Damian Damianov is third. All the national athletes return home with a medal.

The mood is excellent. The hopes are high for the strong performance to be repeated at the World Championships in Vancouver.

***

"I can't lose weight anymore, I will lift in Georgi Markov's category at the World Championships in Vancouver," the 29-year-old weightlifter thought he could not take it further.

"Galabin, are you sure about this? This way you will be competing with Georgi Markov, and your category remains vacant," Plamen Asparuhov replies.

"I won't let you down, I will be ready for records," the Olympic champion assures him.

***

The president of the International Weightlifting Federation, Tamas Ajan, is calm. The Bulgarian domination in weightlifting won't darken the Olympics next year. The Hungarian has just learned there is something wrong with the doping samples from the three biggest Bulgarian stars.

"Mister Asparuhov, Boevski, Vanev and Markov were caught manipulating doping tests," Tamas Ajan reports the message personally.

"Ha ha, are you kidding me?" asks the senior coach of the national team, who arrived in Vancouver with the first weightlifters' party. "How can they be caught, if I haven't given them a thing? This is complete rubbish. Tell me, what have they been caught with?"

"I can't tell you yet, there has been a manipulation. The urine of the three athletes is identical! They are banned from competing," Ajan replies firmly.

***

A day before the flight for Vancouver the second group of national athletes leaves the base in Asenovgrad. All of them are prepared for great achievements. The favourites for gold medals are Galabin Boevski, Georgi Markov and Zlatan Vanev. On the way the telephone rings.

"Zlatan, you, Boevski and Georgi have been caught," says Asparouhov's crying.

"What is going on, why do you call now? We are almost on the plane for Vancouver! This is shocking," The World and European champion doesn't know what to say.

"I know you will have some very hard times after this.

You and Georgi will probably be banned for two years. They promised to lower the bans if you keep quiet. Things are different with Galabin, because he has been caught before."

***

The seats were already occupied on the plane for Vancouver. Surprisingly, Galabin Boevski is there too. He is ready to fight to the end. His loyal friend Georgi Gardev is next to him. Last year he had an operation on his right knee. He gets back in the gym to prepare for the World Championships in Vancouver, but injures his left knee too. He decides to rest, so he can recover for the Olympics next year. He was summoned at the last moment, because the team needed points for team rankings and winning a full set of quotas for Athens. The same applied to Damian Damianov, sitting in the back seats. The weightlifter was called in urgently, even though he hasn't trained for several weeks.

***

"I am innocent, I've taken nothing! Tell me what have I been caught with? My urine is clean. You want to twist my hands and destroy me," Galabin Boevski talks quickly in English.

The chairman of the International weightlifting federation Tamas Ajan is standing in front of him. The Hungarian is scared, because he sees the face of the Bulgarian - ready to kill.

"You are my favourite weightlifter. Keep preparing, we will investigate the case and everything will be fine," the chairman cunningly escapes.

The meeting lasts 15 minutes. Galabin understands what Ajan is saying. His desire to attack a second Olympic title in Athens is enormous. Because of it he grasps this small hope. He reconsiders and decides to wait.

***

The attempts follow one after the other. The Olympic, World and European champion Galabin Boevski is sitting in the grandstand.

"My place is not here," the Bulgarian thinks, as he waits for his old roommate Georgi Gardev to get onto the stage. "I was ready. Everything was fine and eight years later they did it to me again."

"167.5 kg" lights up on the board. Gardev makes his first attempt. He holds the barbell with great difficulty and limps on his way back to the training room. Boevski knows what follows. Gardev will struggle, but Plamen Asparuhov will squeeze and drain him like a lemon. This is the world of weightlifting. You lift while you can. No one thinks of vertebrae fractures and dislocations, torn muscles and tendon tears, dislocated elbows and shoulder joints. They are all part of being a weightlifter.

The first event was over. Gardev makes only one successful attempt. If he lifts the first weight in the second event, he will be placed in the ranking and gain points, with which the national team has a chance of receiving the full Olympic quota. The scenario drafted by Galabin in the stand comes true. Gardev lifts 182.5 kg at his first attempt. The clean and jerk puts a lot more stress on the legs and knees. Galabin hopes his friend will stop here. He knows the risk is huge.

Ten minutes later, Georgi returns. The weights prepared are 5 kg heavier. He fails the first time. One more attempt remains. Gardev lifts the barbell, squats with it, and his leg bends. The pain is excruciating. The Bulgarian can't get up by himself. The medical staff come with a stretcher and carry out the weightlifter. He finished 18th but won points for Bulgaria.

***

The mystery with Boevski, Vanev and Markov's urine brings heated comments from all over the world. Galabin's defence is that he had given his sample in front of four people, and all of them signed for the procedure's validity.

The enemies of the Bulgarian weightlifting school immediately reveal a method, proving how easily it is to manipulate a urine test. According to them the practice used was catheterization. It is very painful, but found to be used to cheat.

Clean urine is inserted in the bladder immediately before the sample, through a catheter. When the time for the test comes, the athlete can calmly fill the vials.

Plamen Asparuhov proves it is absolutely possible for the vials containing the samples to be opened without breaking the cap with hot water. Once the vial is opened, the urine can be switched. After that the same cap can be used to seal it.

***

The last Bulgarian weightlifter at the World Championships in Vancouver is Damian Damianov. He remains 11th in the final rating, but helps the team to win a full quota for the Olympics in Athens. Milen Dobrev (94 kg) grabs the title in the Canadian city. A year later he takes the gold at the games in the Greek capital.

Georgi Gardev is immobilized in hospital. The next day he is to be transported to the airport. The specialist Dr. Tony Georgiev, who will operate on his knee tendons, is waiting for him in Sofia.

"Galab, look where we ended up," Gardev says and smiles in his typical manner.

"Georgi this isn't something new in our sport. Look at Damian, he is barely walking. He is thinking of quitting," Boevski replies.

"I need to go to the bathroom, will you help me get up?" asks the 27 years old Gardev plaintively.

Boevski jumps immediately. He holds his friend very carefully, helps him to get out of bed on one leg, while keeping the other immobilized. Every move is terribly painful. Like two war veterans on their way to the bathroom. Galabin and Gardev never return to the stage.

***

The bans are cruel. Boevski has his competition rights revoked for life. Markov and Vanev are banned for two years. Galabin is furious. The Bulgarian Federation has made a deal without consulting him. According to the secret understanding, the weightlifters accept the bans. As a result the penalty period for Vanev and Markov is decreased to a year and a half, Boevski receives 8 years instead of lifetime ban.

The weightlifter from Knezha doesn't accept this lying down. He starts a lawsuit on his own at the Court of Arbitration for Sports in Lausanne. Tamas Ajan makes an unofficial threat that he will suspend the entire national team from competing if it comes to court. Boevski is relentless and spends tens of thousands of dollars in court costs.

Shortly before Christmas 2004, the Court of Arbitration for Sports gives its verdict:

"After analysing all the facts the judges have decided: There is no proof that the caps of the vials containing the urine samples have been opened. On the contrary. The judges united behind the opinion, that the manipulation was made prior or during the urination. Boevski manipulated his sample by himself, or with the help of others. Therefore the court confirms the 8-years ban."

CHAPTER IX

The police car has just left Itai prison. Galabin throws a last look out through the van's barred window. He left two years of his life there. But all this was part of the past. After a few hours he will fly off from Brazil. His right hand slides down his leg. His fingers pinch his thigh as hard as they can. It is true. It was all over.

Four hours later in Sao Paulo airport the police officers are standing at his side. They have to take him to the departure terminal. The legendary weightlifter turns back. It is the same madhouse as last time. Then the whole world turned upside down. He forces these thoughts away. On his left he sees two Africans without luggage. Their colourful shirts are very popular in Brazil. It seemed as if they were communicating through their eyes. Immediately Galabin knew they were dealing in drugs. He had seen dozens like them in prison and was able to recognise them right away. Behind bars he found out that the Africans were part of a well-worked scheme for suitcase swapping. In it were airport employees, customs, and even police.

"No, that's enough," Galabin puts an end to these thoughts. He was leaner in the face. On the other hand, the muscles in his body were still strong. He wanted to walk faster so that he could calm down. In the distance, he saw a familiar silhouette. A thin woman with a pony tail. His wife Krasimira. The person who never left him. She risked a lot coming to Brazil. Not only herself, but also her two daughters – Myra and Sarah. The little one was also at the airport, as the older one had gone home a couple of weeks earlier. Myra saw him first. She froze for a couple of seconds next to her mother as if to recognise him and discard all doubts that he was finally out of that horrid place. The small feet rushed towards him. Galabin picked her up. It was the most pleasant weight he had lifted in his entire life.

***

The sports minister and one of the most famous Bulgarian businessmen Vasil Ivanov loved cars, dining with people he knew and didn't know, and paying the whole bill. He had the nickname Luciano, because he liked dressing as the legendary Italian mobster. He had befriended the chairman of the Bulgarian Olympic Committee Ivan "Bateto" Slavkov. The two of them were typical bohemians. There were those who looked for their negative sides, but most, even today, only have good things to say about Luciano and Bateto.

Vasil Ivanov was sports minister in the Simeon Saxe-Coburg-Gotha's government. In his typical manner he helped those, whom he saw worthy of helping. He gave 30 000 euros towards the trial of Galabin Boevski against the International Weightlifting Federation in the Arbitration Court in Lausanne. He organised another kindness for the weightlifter. He gave him a room in the "Vasil Levski" stadium at a symbolic monthly rent after the doping scandal of the World Championships in Vancouver. The small hall became a gym, named "Boevski 2000"

***

"Paul, come on, you are going to miss practice," Galabin urged on his son. The weightlifter is standing next to the family's Toyota, which has replaced the sold Mercedes.

"I am coming, I am coming," replies the 11-year-old Paul, as he rushes out of their house in the capital's "Borovo" district. The boy carries a small bag, in which he has the white strip of the "Slavia" football team.

In the autumn of 2003 the Olympic champion bought his first own home in Sofia. With the money saved through the years, the weightlifter had finally provided security for his family. His neighbour was Plamen Asparuhov, who was still coach of the national team. Relations between them were cold for a while. The reason was Galabin's hatred of the chairman of the Federation Anton Kodzhabashev, who didn't do a thing to support him in Vancouver.

***

All of Knezha is talking about the hottest topic. Galabin Boevski is opening a luxurious café in town. It's called "Dreams & Realities". The name is dedicated to the entire career of the weightlifter and the long talks he had with Hristo Boev after each training session. It was the coach himself, who took up the building of the house, on the first floor of which was the café. The money was found by hard work.

"Galabin, there was a good profit in buying the tractor and harvester," Hristo Boev, who operated the machines himself, says smiling. "The café will be dedicated to you."

"Big Brother, I want you to manage it. I won't be around, because we will be with the children in Sofia. You know they go to school there. I trust you completely."

At the beginning of 2013 the partnership crumbles.

Lawsuits begin between Hristo Boev and the Boevski family. The reason is the need for money, to finance the court expenses of Galabin in Brazil. The coach withdraws offended from the café partnership.

***

"Why don't you try politics? Look how popular you are. You are friends with Luciano, everybody knows you," Georgi Gardev drives on his friend.

They were sitting in the gym of the "Vasil Levski" stadium. The effect of the operation has not yet passed. Gardev instinctively massages his knee from time to time. He could feel the head of the 10-centimeters nail, inserted there.

"All is clear in politics," Galabin replied. "It's not for me. You have to have stable positions. How do you think a man gets to be a member?"

"Galab, you know your stuff, I'm just saying. Check this guy out – Boiko Borisov, why don't you try to find your way to him. He looks like a decent guy."

Boevski smiled, but remembered the conversation.

***

"Galabin, I have problems," the sad look of Boevski's first coach – Stefcho Malkodanski dived into the eyes of his former student. They were sitting in a café near the "Vasil Levski" stadium. "I haven't come to you, because you became famous or because you have money. I need an operation. I have heart problems. Will you help me? I swear that all those years I trained you the Federation gave me only 500 levs."

"I was a student and a weightlifter," the newly made businessman replied firmly. "You were a coach. It was your job to school and mentor me. Mine – to lift and compete. I owe you nothing. You should have abandoned me. Nobody forced you to protect me and take me to tournaments."

"Do you remember the things we went through together?" Stefcho Malkodanski waxes sentimental. "Do you remember how we got robbed in Germany? How I transferred you from "Olympic Hopes" to Pleven? How I got you to train in weightlifting?"

"There is no need to remind me of everything we've been through," The former athlete didn't lower his eyes. "I never asked you to help me. Goodbye, Krasimira is waiting."

Boevski left. Stefcho Malkodanski paid for his coffee and sadly shook his head.

***

"Gardev, you made a wonderful self-sacrifice at the World Championships. I will appoint you assistant-coach to Plamen Asparuhov until the Olympics," the president of the Federation, Anton Kodzhabashev, raised his hand as a gesture of favour towards the injured weightlifter.

"But I can't even walk normally yet, it would be very difficult for me," the hero from Vancouver excused himself.

"Don't worry. Rest, recover and call me after," the businessman from Bourgas confirmed.

***

Boevski's hatred towards the president of the Weightlifting Federation Anton Kodzhabashev grows. The Olympic champion travels through the country with a petition calling for the convening of a general meeting of the Weightlifting Federation. The goal is the removal of the management.

Immediately before the European Championships in Kiev, during the spring of the Olympic year, Gardev is already prepared to take on his duties. His bags are packed, but at the last moment Kodzhabashev tells him to wait. After a couple of months, the hero from Vancouver is in Sofia to speak with the boss of the Federation personally.

"I can no longer appoint you Asparuhov's assistant, you can eventually become trainer of the juniors," Kodzhabashev breaks the deal.

Later on, Gardev's scholarship, which continues to be paid while he is recovering, is stopped.

"What is going on? Why don't I have any money?" The former national athlete calls the Federation's chairman.

"There is no money! And there won't be any!" Kodzhabashev is firm. "You are Galabin's friend, right? You are calling for a general meeting to get rid of me. I can't support my enemies."

"I have been friends with him for a long time. If you are looking at things in that way, why didn't you give me an Olympic bonus, which you gave him after Sydney? What happened to all the big talk after Vancouver?" Gardev continued to insist.

"I have decided this, and that's the way it's going to be," the Federation's chairman is like a rock. "Life is a boomerang – it flies, flies, flies, hits you hard and it hurts. You are still young, but sooner or later you will understand that."

***

The Olympics in Athens are successful for Bulgarian weightlifting. Milen Dobrev wins a title. Velichko Cholakov finishes third. Nevertheless the clubs in Bulgaria are unhappy. At the general meeting there are four candidates for chairman – the present chief Anton Kodzhabashev, Galabin Boevski, Andon Nikolov and, returning from Australia, former national athlete, Stefan Botev.

On the election day, Tamas Ajan, the head of world

weightlifting, who made the deal about Galabin, Vanev and Markov last year with Kodzhabashev, sends a telegram. In it, he says the International Weightlifting Federation does not approve of the application of a man, who was involved with doping. Boevski pulls out, but transfers all his votes to Andon Nikolov. The Olympic champion from Munich '72 and former assistant to Ivan Abadzhiev in the national team overthrow Kodzhabashev.

Neno Terziiski is elected the new national team coach. Georgi Gardev becomes his assistant. Stefan Botev takes on the office of general secretary of the Federation. Boevski receives a position on the Executive Board and Andon Nikolov's promise that no important decisions would be taken without his approval.

***

"What is going on? Why are you leaving?" Georgi Gardev met Galabin at the door. Behind him the New Year's banquet of the Weightlifting Federation is beginning. Music sounds from the restaurant of the "Diana" hotel. A while ago the meeting of the Executive Board had been held in the same place.

"I am leaving. I have resigned from the Executive Board. I put this guy there, and I will remove him," Boevski spits out. The object of his hatred is the new chairman of the Federation Andon Nikolov.

From this moment on attitudes change towards Gardev. Everyone thinks of him as Boevski's man and tries to isolate him. Moreover, Andon Nikolov doesn't allow the former World and European silver medalist to start his own club in Pazardzhik. He is worried Gardev's vote could help bring about an eventual coup against him.

***

"Georgi, I am going to the foundation of the GERB party," states Galabin, who now has new plans for his future. During the last few years he has distanced himself from weightlifting and focused his efforts on business.

"I thought you don't want to go into politics," Gardev smiles.

"I met Boiko Borisov and we have agreed on some interesting things about sport," Boevski adds.

In the autumn of 2007 Boiko Borisov wins a second term as mayor of Sofia. Galabin gains a place on the new city council. He also receives the prestigious position of chairman of the commission of children, youth and sports. The GERB party becomes the most popular in the country and is favourite for the parliament elections in 2009.

"Sharpen your wits, because Boiko is grooming you for sports minister," the former high official Vasil "Luciano" Ivanov confides to Galabin at one of their meetings.

***

For a one year Galabin's business goes very well. He also takes his first steps in politics. His two older children have already gone their own way. Paul is transferred from the youth team of "Slavia" to the most popular football club "Levski", despite his father being a great fan of Levski's prime rival – CSKA. Sarah has been training for tennis. Galabin feels his home is getting emptier. He knows the apartment in Borovo will be empty in a couple of years. The third child of Galabin and Krasimira is born on the 12th of February, 2008. The weightlifter and his wife planned Myra's birth.

***

"It is not my son's fault, that two boys put a gun to his head and shot him!" Boevski shouts at a teacher at the "William Gladstone" school in Sofia. Earlier in the day the weightlifter had received the bad news that his son has been shot with a gas pistol in the head.

"Every other student gave written statements, saying your son was carrying the gun in his backpack. It was started by him. Besides he had pointed it at a teacher's back, while she was writing on the board," answers the school master.

Galabin's reaction is ugly. His insults and threats towards the teachers were documented in a declaration sent directly to Sofia's mayor, Boiko Borisov. All 147 teachers and employees sign it, requesting Galabin Boevski's resignation from the city council.

The former weightlifter had already given it. He finishes with politics exactly six months after he got in it.

"What Paul has done, I have to deal with alone," Galabin says to his relatives.

***

Boevski sees in his son Paul his own rebellious character. The boy surpasses his father, despite living in a calmer environment.

"If you only knew what I have been through," Boevski senior thought, as he was considering Paul's punishment after his latest mischief. No word, nor forbidance had any effect on the boy, whose greatest passion is football. To keep him out of trouble Galabin drives him every day to the "Levski" football team's stadium and takes him back after practice.

Bulgaria's media pour extra gasoline on the flames. The yellow press portray Boevski's son as a monster. Alcohol, drugs, and fornication – everything is slapped on the young football player.

Boevski isn't spared. "Galabin threw his son out", and "Boevski was beating his kids for every mistake they made," thunder from the online editions, aiming to smear the name of the strong family.

Paul does not deal with the pressure. The problems reflect on his performance on the football field. His talent is never confirmed at "Levski". The manager of the big football star Dimitar Berbatov – Emil Danchev, arranges for Paul to go to the German team "Freiburg". Galabin's son only lasts a short time there. At the end of 2013 Paul returns to Knezha. He works as a bartender in his family's café "Dreams & Realities", now managed by his grandmother Stella.

***

The death knell for Bulgarian weightlifting sounds in the summer of 2008. The entire team, preparing for the Olympics in Beijing, is caught with doping. Anabolic steroids are found in the weightlifters' urine. The team's coach Plamen Asparuhov swears his innocence. All national athletes think it's a conspiracy.

Galabin's old competitor Georgi Markov is banned for life. Another of his teammates from the Sydney Olympics, Alan Tsagaev, receives the same punishment. The other athletes are banned for four years. The Bulgarian Weightlifting Federation basically ceases to exist. After the scandal, the team's next participation in the World Championships is in 2013.

***

"Galabin, send me Sarah for training, I want to make up a children's group," offers the tennis coach Misho Andreev, after another game on the courts of the Library Institute. "You play tennis. Paul, too. May be she can get hooked too. She can come twice a week."

The girl is only ten years old at the time.

Three tennis seasons later Sarah, who took after her father, has grown stronger. She shows excellent qualities, and the strict Galabin is by her side at every tournament.

"It's difficult for me with the tennis," Galabin Boevski admits to his former roommate in the national team Georgi Gardev. "These trips abroad are very expensive. When she gets onto the main tournaments it will repay itself a hundred fold. You know how it was with Maria Sharapova and her father, who invested a lot and kept her in line.

Paul, Myra, Krasimira and Sarah (from left to right)

Tennis circles are shocked by the father's behaviour. At a tournament on the courts in Sliven, next to the famous football player Yordan Lechkov's hotel, Galabin's anger falls on the umpire. The threats are fierce. Sarah is in danger of a serious ban and suspension of competition rights.

**

The most luxurious gym on Sofia opens its doors in May, 2010. The complex, carrying the Olympic champion's name "2fit by Boevski", is spread through a vast area of 1600 square meters. The machines are brand new and modern. The interior would make the residents of Beverly Hills jealous.

The owner of the establishment is the company "M-Unite". Galabin owns 50% of it. The other partner with 50% is Milena Boeva. During the first year the gym is on the edge of bankruptcy, due to the high rent and expenses. There are not many customers, but Boevski's name and the quality of service have their effect. The sports complex starts working properly and makes a profit. At the end of 2012, Milena Boeva sends a warning letter to the former weightlifter about leaving the company. According to it, the businesswoman's partner was performing activities damaging to the company's interests and acted in terms of unfair competition. Galabin is unable to react, because at that time he is in jail. The court decides for him to be removed from the "M-Unite" company.

**

Shortly before opening the gym, Galabin Boevski starts another enterprise with the businesswoman Iva Ivanova. He registers the "Scandal V.I.P." company, and rents the former striptease bar "Angels" in the "Sheraton" Hotel. The thematic furnishings are preserved and the company runs ads for hiring new erotic dancers.

At the beginning of 2013 the club lives up to its name. Police from Bulgaria's specialized forces for counteracting organized crime storm the bar. They arrest four men and one woman for procuring. One of them – Valeri Popov, is identified as the leader. He is a former partner of Galabin in the "Scandal V.I.P." company, who later sells his share to Iva Ivanova. Others are Tsvetan Timanov, Sefan Marev, Georgi Andreev and Gergana Lazarova. Boevski is not part of the case, because at the time he is still in jail in Brazil.

***

At the start of 2013 Galabin's fellow citizen – Matey Milkov Boev is summoned by the court in Milan. He is accused of being the primary middleman in Switzerland, laundering the assets of the drug boss Evelin "Brendo" Banev. Italian prosecutors uncover that Boev used the accounts of the cocaine mobster, who was extradited to Italy in 2012.

Matey is Milena Boeva's husband. A year later she has appropriated the gym on "Tsarigradsko shose" in Sofia from Galabin Boevski. Her name also appears in the Italian police investigation as Brendo's partner.

CHAPTER X

"Dad, can I get an ice cream?" Sarah asked as they approached the gate at "Guarughos" airport in Sao Paulo. There was still enough time until the flight of "Iberia" airlines to Madrid.

"Of course," Galabin Boevski replied.

He reached in his pocket for his last reals. They won't be needing them anymore. In the morning the two of them left the town of Itajai, where his daughter had a girls tennis tournament. They got the first of three flights to Bulgaria from the bigger city of Navegantes. Galabin wanted to check in all the suitcases straight to Sofia, but was told it was not possible. He would have to do it in Sao Paulo. Before lunch Boevski and Sarah decided to complete the job, they passed through passport control and were now able to calmly wait for the departure to Madrid.

"Can I see your passports?" A federal police officer turned to Galabin with a firm voice. The cop was accompanied by another officer with a badge.

Boevski and Sarah handed over their passports and looked at each other.

"Please come with us," The federal officer said firmly.

Galabin turned to the board with departing flights. He saw the date – 24th of October 2011 and the precise time – 14:30.

***

"Is this your suitcase?" The Brazilian policeman asked. "The dog has scented something in it."

"It is ours by the look of it," the former weightlifter replied.

The policeman opened the briefcase and took out the clothes. There was nothing else in it. Then he took a screwdriver and tore the suitcase. A bag of white powder fell out. The federal officer smiling looked at the Bulgarians. Sarah's eyes filled with tears.

***

Galabin thought over the day while waiting in the airport's detention room. It all started when he decided to change the suitcases, because Sarah's old duffel bag was damaged. The tennis tournament's photographer recommended a local mall and even drove them there. There was a shop selling suitcases at low prices. The weightlifter bought a set of three, delivered to the hotel.

Neither Sarah, nor Galabin discovered anything wrong when receiving them.

***

"I don't know anything," Sarah says in tears, after the policemen started his questioning again.

The girl was upset, because she was separated from her father.

"We are certain you do," the Brazilian federal police continued. "If you don't tell us we will send you to a place where they rape and then kill pretty young girls like you.

There you will find under aged criminals and who are not afraid of anything."

"I don't know anything, we bought the suitcases from a mall and they were delivered to the hotel." Sarah tries to convince the policemen in the secret hope they would let her father go.

The promising fifteen years old tennis player spends the night in a boarding house. The next day she is put on a plane without a guardian for Bulgaria. Galabin remained in jail.

***

"I have never committed a crime," Galabin confides in an interview for Bulgaria's national television a few weeks after his detention. "I bought three brand new suitcases, and they were absolutely empty. My biggest problem is that they ruined my good name, which I have spent many years building. I am popular enough everywhere. I am an Olympic champion, and would be mad to do something like that. There is enough money for me to live on without doing stupid things like that. I hope to be released soon, to help resolve the whole situation. I have a good life and a good business. I don't need to do things like that."

***

Krasimira arrived in Brazil in the second week of Galabin's detention. She started organizing his defence right away. She consulted every part of the case with the Bulgarian lawyer Ivaylo Dermendzhiev. He was the one fighting the weightlifter's lawsuit in the Court of Arbitration for Sports after the scandal at the World Championships in Vancouver.

Krasimira also hired the Brazilian attorney Leonardo Pereira, who focused mainly on two things – the suitcase shop's security camera footage, and tracing the

The three suitcases that were bought by Boevski in Brazil

Itai prison is home to 1500 criminals

weightlifter's phone calls. The suitcases were mysteriously damaged beyond recognition while being stored as evidence in the case. Due to this negligence there was no way of determining if they had been interfered with by a third party, what brand they were or who was the manufacturer.

During the trial the attorney for the defence entered a not guilty plea. The nine kilograms of cocaine in the suitcase were explained as him being "the involuntary victim of a drug trafficking canal for Europe".

***

The judge Maria Isabel do Prado did not accept the mobile phone tracing and the shop's security camera footage as evidence. She rejected the weightlifter's excuse of not knowing about the cocaine, because he would have felt the weight in the new suitcase.

"His reputation as a sports celebrity, as well as his social status, call for him to be guilty if he does not have manners higher than the average standards, as his enhanced personal status calls for him to observe conditions where he abides by the laws of the state," was the explanation of the sentence.

The verdict was one of the heaviest for this amount of drug offence – 9 years and 4 months. The decision in the first instance was given on May 3rd, 2012.

***

The three federal officers operated the procedure to the last letter. They had a list with names of prisoners in Itaí, whom they had to enquire about. The list was issued every couple of months, and included prisons in all Brazilian states. The officers didn't know how the names ended up on it. Sometimes there were a lot, other times fewer. They were all foreigners, some of them convicted of murder, others for rape, but the drug smugglers were the biggest category of all.

If they met the conditions, the interviewees would receive an "expulsao" document, granting them extradition regardless of how much time they had left until the end of their sentence.

The rules were clear. The people on the list had to give their fingerprints, a cast of their teeth and have their tattoos photographed.

The Bulgarian Galabin Pepov Boevski was next to answer the questions. They were asked by the head federal officer.

"Do you wish to remain here in Brazil, or go back to your country?" The policeman asked.

"I want to go back to Bulgaria, there is nothing for me here," Galabin Boevski replied seriously.

He knew how important answering the questions correctly without hesitation was. He was prepared for this trial by the two new attorneys, replacing Leonardo Pereira – Jackson Nilo de Paula and Marcos Gomes.

"The procedure for issuing an "expulsao" by the Ministry of Justice lasts several months," the federal officer explained. "Then the judge has to sign it and you will be extradited in a couple of days. The Ministry of Justice will buy you a ticket to your country and you will be escorted to the airport. You will not be permitted to come back to Brazil for the next five years."

***

The classroom was the best place in the whole prison. In it was a board, a few chairs and book shelves. It was next to the library.

Galabin was patiently waiting. Twenty minutes ago the guard told him the journalists had arrived. A month and a half ago the prison's officials asked him if he wanted to give an interview for the magazine reporting on the Olympics in Rio de Janeiro in 2016. The weightlifter agreed at first, but then changed his mind. He knew they would not ask him about his incredible records and dozens of medals from the world's biggest competitions. But there was no going back, because the correspondent was coming from Sao Paulo.

The journalist's name was Larissa. She was about 30 years old. A translator and a veteran photographer were accompanying her. It turned out the reporter's initial idea was to write an article on training in prison. She got a reply, stating there was a former elite Bulgarian weightlifter in Itai, who was well known 10–15 years ago. After permission from the Ministry of Justice and prison authorities was given, the Brazilian and her team entered the room.

***

The procedure for entering the prison turned out to be harder than expected. Larissa and Frederic Jean were frisked closely. The Brazilian was ready for anything, after putting so much effort into getting to the Bulgarian weightlifter. She was very well prepared. She used Google's translating service to investigate everything about the life of the Olympic champion. The articles were in the thousands, and the interest of the Bulgarian media in him was enormous.

The subject of the interview seemed in good shape. He was lean, with muscles evident. He was obviously working out. His beard and hair had been cut, with nails trimmed and clean. Larissa was surprised when she looked Galabin Boevski in the eyes. His eyebrows had most likely been plucked. The journalist could not help smiling. She knew this was not common practice for men in Brazil. After all this was prison.

Her countrymen didn't look kindly at this sort of

vanity. For Brazilians such behaviour was too feminine for a man. The combination of the world's strongest weightlifter and plucked eyebrows was unexpected for the journalist. She swallowed and focused on the first question.

***

Larissa turned the recorder on, and marked the date in the notebook – July 22th, 2013. She had prepared several lines of conversation. Minute after minute the Brazilian was not getting what she wanted. Galabin was refusing to speak about the scandalous moments in his career, and troubles with his son. His answers were vague. On top of all that the translator was speaking with the weightlifter in Bulgarian, but giving one sentence replies in Portuguese.

Larissa took a deep breath. She realized this would be the most difficult interview of her life. She had talked with ministers, governors, mayors, angry people, foreigners, and blind people, but things were not going well here.

The Brazilian looked at her interlocutor again. She had uncovered a lot about him. He was definitely a rude person, but this could be in some way be justified by the situation he was in. He had seen a lot in his life – doping scandals, the trouble with his son, and the arrest for drug smuggling in a foreign country. "Does this make him a bad person?" she asked herself. She started looking for an excuse for every action that had led Galabin to prison.

The journalist had no idea of the situation the man in front of her was in, to make the decision to travel in distant South America. The Brazilian didn't consider he might be innocent. His suitcase story sounded quite naïve.

"I won't justify him," Larissa promised herself and wrote something in her notebook. "One thing is certain – he has definitely made wrong decisions in his life. He is also quite arrogant."

She remembered another interesting fact. While

preparing the documents for the interview, she contacted the Bulgarian embassy. She asked them to contact Galabin Boevski's wife – Krasimira. In the beginning the woman was ready to speak and present all the required documents proving her husband's innocence, but then she changed her mind. In the email correspondence, Galabin's wife stated several times she believed the weightlifter.

***

Forty minutes after the beginning of the interview Larissa decided to end the farce. Galabin Boevski's ironic look was indicating he had nothing more to say. The last and most important task in the whole interview remained. The weightlifter showed himself to be a fool once again – he refused to be photographed.

Luckily the journalist took with her the magazine's best photographer. The veteran Frederic Jean knew what to do. It took quite a lot of time to convince the Bulgarian. His only condition was that he was not to be photographed in a prison environment.

"The miracle has happened," Larissa thought while looking at the former weightlifter's happy face. She had no idea that on the 31st of March Galabin Boevski had received an "expulsao". It was just a matter of time before the federal judge signed his extradition.

***

"We received a message from the prison in Itai. Galabin Boevski is free," employees of the Bulgarian ambassador in Brazil Chavdar Nikolov reported to him. "They drove him to the airport for extradition three hours ago."

The diplomat looked at the clock. It showed 16:00, and the date was the 22nd of October. It was almost midnight in Bulgaria. Even if he sent the telegram immediately it would not be read until the next day.

Chavdar Nikolov reflected on the circumstances. He recalled that just 11 days ago Galabin Boevski had asked for a temporary passport. That piece of paper was needed for him to start a job while he was doing his time.

***

While looking at the Internet edition of "O Globo" newspaper, the journalist Larissa Veloso came upon a familiar name. Her interviewee from three months ago, Galabin Boevski had surprisingly returned home.

She could not believe the weightlifter had left the country so quickly. She remembered the conversation with the Bulgarian's two attorneys. They were certain Boevski would have to serve his sentence to the end, before extradition. Apparently people in the weightlifter's country were surprised too. The commentary said that due to his mysterious return, of which no one had been informed, they had fired Bulgaria's ambassador to Brazil Chavdar Nikolov.

***

The plane from Paris had left for Bulgaria. Galabin felt like a free man. There were two more hours until landing. Krasimira and Myra were with him. Paul and Sarah waited at home. His mother Stella was going to meet him at the airport.

Memories from the last two years came into his mind. They merged together, as hope and despair had walked hand in hand in prison. He remembered a book that was filled with wisdom. It said the key to failure is trying to be liked by everybody. This was his life's motto set to words years after he had achieved so much. He managed to leave the small town of Knezha and prove himself. He was declared Bulgaria's greatest champion of all sports. He won an Olympic title. He broke world records, won gold medals for his country. He raised a family with three children, bought an apartment, had a successful business…

He knew whatever he said people in Bulgaria wouldn't believe him.

It wasn't important to him. He hoped the people who loved, respected and knew him would find out the truth.

***

Stella was waiting, obscured by the vast group of welcoming people. The flight from Paris had arrived. The passengers were coming out, but her son wasn't there. It was as if the heart of the worried woman missed a beat. She was really concerned. Her eyes were wet when she saw Myra, Krasimira and Galabin. Her boy seemed to have lost weight, but basically was unchanged. Stella got up and walked towards him. At that moment she saw the camera of Bulgaria's national television. She thought for a second and decided not to complicate things. She knew they won't be able to talk at that moment. From a distance she followed Galabin, Krasimira and Myra as the reporters crowded around them. They got in a taxi.

"That was Galabin Boevski, he has arrived," one of the taxi drivers forwarded the news. "Who picked him up, and will he drive him all the way to Knezha?"

"Bravo, he's welcome, let them fete him." The buzz from Sofia Airport's event of the day continued.

Stella took another taxi. She gave the address in the "Borovo" district. The thirty minutes to the apartment went very slowly. The woman tidied her short hair as she left the yellow vehicle. She went into the apartment. He was there, waiting for her. He hugged Stella, who started sobbing loudly.

"Mother, I'm alive. I don't want you to cry!" Galabin said quietly, holding his widowed mother in his strong arms.

The white prisoner – Galabin Boevski's secret story

ABOUT THE AUTHOR

Ognian Georgiev is a sport journalist, who is currently working as sports editor at the "Bulgaria Today" daily newspaper. He covered the Summer Olympics in Beijing 2008 and in London 2012.

The author specializes in sports politics, investigations and coverage of Olympic sports events.

Ognian Georgiev works as a TV broadcaster for Eurosport Bulgaria, Nova Broadcasting group, TV+, F+ and TV7. He is a commentator for fight sports events such as boxing/kickboxing and MMA.

The author was born in the capital city of Bulgaria - Sofia. He started work as a sports reporter in 2000. In the following years Ognian Georgiev covered different sports events in USA, Germany, Switzerland, UK, France, Greece, Serbia, Hungary, Spain, and Italy.

The author lives in Sofia with his partner Ralitza and their one year old daughter Valeria.

You may find more about the book on Facebook:

https://www.facebook.com/galabin.boevsky
Twitter: https://twitter.com/galabinboevski
Web page: http://ogigeorgiev.wordpress.com

GRATITUDE

I would like to express my gratitude to the many people who have provided support, talked things over, read, written, offered comments, allowed me to quote and assisted in the editing, proofreading and design.

I would like to give many thanks to my editor in chief Nikolay Penchev, with whom I shared the idea to write the book. I want to thank the entire team of my Bulgarian publisher "Trud" for their hard work. I received a great deal of respect from Galabin Boevski's relatives, his mother, his trainers over the years, his teammates from the national team, journalists and many others, who allowed me to tell those unique stories, on which the book was based.

Many thanks to my friends Vasil Koynarev and Lili Kaneva, who inspired me to prepare the English edition of the book. I very much appreciate the efforts of my translator Ilko Germanov, my English editor Chris Feetam and cover illustrator Velizar Stefanov. Thank you guys!

The English version would not be the same without the amazing help from my test readers Randall J Strossen, Gregor Winter, Bob Takano, Greg Everett, Richard Pound, Slawomir Judek, Arthur Chidlovski, Grit Hartmann, Nadya Koseva, Rich Kite, Joe Micela, Alan Abrahamson, Alex Kaneva, Daniel Rosen and Nat Arem.

Last and not least, thanks for all the support from my girlfriend Ralitza and my one-year-old daughter Valeria. I was away from home for some weeks, researching and writing the story, but they never complained and with their sweet smiles always encouraged me at the most difficult moments.

Made in the USA
Lexington, KY
31 August 2014